T0276417

AROUND THE
WORLD
IN
80
BIRDS

First published in Great Britain in 2022 by
Laurence King an imprint of
The Orion Publishing Group Ltd
Carmelite House
50 Victoria Embankment
London EC4Y 0DZ

An Hachette UK Company

10 9 8 7 6 5 4 3 2

Text © 2022 Mike Unwin

Mike Unwin has asserted his right under the Copyright,
Designs, and Patents Act 1988, to be identified as the author
of this work.

Illustrations © 2022 Ryuto Miyake

Ryuto Miyake has asserted his right under the Copyright,
Designs, and Patents Act 1988, to be identified as the author
of the illustrations.

All rights reserved. No part of this publication may be
reproduced, stored in a retrieval system, or transmitted in
any form or by any means, electronic, mechanical, photocopy,
recording or otherwise, without the prior permission of both
the copyright owner and the above publisher of the book.

A CIP catalogue record for this book is available from
the British Library.

Senior editor: Melissa Mellor
Design: Masumi Briozzo
Cover design: Florian Michelet
Cover illustrations: Ryuto Miyake

ISBN: 978-0-85782-895-8

Origination by DL Imaging, UK
Printed in China by C&C Offset Printing Co. Ltd

Laurence King is committed to ethical and sustainable
production. We are proud participants in
The Book Chain Project
bookchainproject.com

www.laurenceking.com
www.orionbooks.co.uk

AROUND THE
WORLD
IN
80
BIRDS

Mike Unwin

Illustrations by Ryuto Miyake

Laurence King Publishing

Contents

Introduction

It's 7.45 am and already birds have stamped themselves on my day: over breakfast, the chime of a great tit and machine-gun rattle of magpies from the garden; now, upstairs at my desk, the mewling of herring gulls drifting past my window. My tiny urban patch is hardly a bird reserve and yet by the end of an average working day, including a lunchtime stroll around the park, I will generally have seen or heard some 25 species. Add to that the profusion of avian imagery that I am bound to encounter – from book spines to tattoos – and it's clear that there is no escaping birds.

This is hardly surprising, given how numerous birds are. Taxonomists continue to debate the precise number of species, with new DNA-based classification systems overturning traditional morphological ones, but a total somewhere north of 11,000 is now widely accepted. Compared with some 6,400 species of mammal and 10,000 reptiles, this makes Aves probably the most diverse of all vertebrate classes.

Of course, these species are not evenly distributed. The richest habitat for birds is tropical forest, which explains why six of the world's top ten bird-rich nations are in northern South America, with Colombia (home to over 1,950 species) being number one. However, there is nowhere that does not have its own avifauna. The extraordinary versatility of birds as a group has enabled them to conquer the most hostile landscapes, from deserts and mountains to ice-caps and the open ocean. Their ability to fly leaves no corner of the planet out of reach – and allows them to escape harsh winters or seasonal food shortages by simply migrating to pastures new.

But it's not just about numbers. While most mammals are small and nocturnal, and most reptiles hidden away under rocks or leaf litter, birds are noisy, colourful and conspicuously present in every sphere of our daily lives. As a child growing up in a UK town, my imagination may have been teased by pythons and polar bears in distant lands, but it was the local birdlife that I could actually see, and thus the much more real possibility of glimpsing my first kingfisher or barn owl that lured me out into nature and inspired a lifetime passion for the natural world.

The in-your-face ubiquity of birds may explain why they have generated more research and inspired more art over the centuries than any other faunal group. In science, they have been the gateway to our understanding of such fundamental concepts as evolution (think Darwin's finches). In culture, they have spawned endless music, art and literature, and become emblematic of everything from military might to spiritual transcendence. From Noah's dove to the sacred quetzal of the Aztecs, every society has held up birds of one kind or another as mirrors to its own values and beliefs.

This book tells the stories of 80 bird species, each representing a country or territory where it finds a particular significance. The selection aims to showcase the diversity of the avian world. It includes household favourites, ocean wanderers, formidable raptors and tropical beauties. But rather than being an identification guide or coffee-table gallery, this book is more concerned with what the birds mean to us. Each species is described not only in terms of its natural history but also in the context of its relationship with humankind, whether cultural, historical or scientific.

Whittling down my selection to 80 species was a thorny challenge. I could as easily have chosen 80 others – and you may be puzzled or disappointed that such perennial favourites as peregrine falcon and peacock didn't make the final cut, or that I failed to accommodate a single heron or woodpecker. But my dilemma, I hope, simply emphasizes the breadth of riches on offer.

Across the list, it is clear that birds grab our interest and attention through certain consistent factors. First, of course, is basic visual impact. For the Malayan peacock-pheasant, it is simply exquisite plumage that wows us. Many birds flaunt their finery in dramatic displays: the Andean cock-of-the-rock and the superb bird-of-paradise leap out, literally, in this respect. And we are often grabbed as much by the bizarre as the beautiful: take the inflated air sacs of a displaying greater sage grouse or the preposterous lance of a sword-billed hummingbird.

But the appeal isn't only visual. Birds also have voices, which excite both our ears and our imaginations, encouraging us to attribute to them meanings of our own. The complex melody of a common nightingale has become imbued with lyrical romance while the hoarse *kronk* of a raven is associated with death. And nothing can evoke place quite like the call of a bird, whether the Canadian wilderness embodied in the quavering wail of a common loon or the dusty Australian outback captured in the cackle of a kookaburra.

The extraordinary things birds do also inspire us. We applaud the skill of a tailorbird stitching its leaf-cradle or the collective industry of sociable weavers constructing their haystack apartment block. We marvel at the torrent duck raising its chicks in a foaming Andean cataract or the greater honeyguide leading honey gatherers to a bees' nest. And we gasp with incredulity at the male emperor penguin that incubates an egg on its feet above the Antarctic ice or the common swift that can stay airborne for over a year without once touching down.

Among this astounding variety, some bird species have found their lives interwoven with our own. These include those that we have harvested as a resource, whether for their meat, eggs or feathers, or have exploited through domestication on a vast scale – none more so than the domestic hen, whose wild red junglefowl ancestor still roams the forests of southern Asia. They also include synanthropic species that have adapted to the human landscape, from alpine choughs flocking to Swiss ski resorts to purple martins adopting multi-storey nest boxes in American backyards.

The most celebrated among all these species are those that we have elevated to cultural icons, bringing an anthropomorphic take to their perceived attributes, such as beauty, strength or intelligence. Thus, species as diverse as the purple-crested turaco (Eswatini) and brahminy kite (India) have acquired royal or even divine associations in their respective parts of the world, while others, such as the kiwi and bald eagle, are universally recognized as national emblems, embodying the pride of an entire nation.

There is also a more disturbing factor that has earned some birds their place in this book: their rarity. For each of my 80 species, I have included the conservation status assigned by the International Union for Conservation of Nature (IUCN), ranging from Least Concern to Critically Endangered. Several, such as Gurney's pitta and the kakapo, have flirted so perilously with extinction that they are famous for this reason alone and now highlight the catastrophic impact of humankind on the world's birdlife. Over the last 500 years we have driven at least 150 species to extinction and today around one in eight is endangered. The causes range from persecution to trade, but above all birds have suffered from our continued trashing of their natural habitats, whether through deforestation, agriculture, urbanization, pollution, invasive alien species or – potentially the most devastating threat of all – climate change.

Today, conservation is doing its bit. And a growth in public interest means there is, at least, the will to act. The conspicuous nature of birds means that their plight is hard to ignore: the disappearance of much-loved species from our countryside or the grim litter of oiled seabirds on our beaches touches many. It also means that birds are often the first to alert us to wider threats. In the 1960s, for example, it was the decline of the peregrine falcon that first alerted scientists to the devastation caused by the insecticide DDT in the food chain. By protecting birds, we are thus protecting the natural environment for everything else – including ourselves.

Birds also offer gifts that are less tangible but no less significant: gifts such as companionship, pleasure and psychological well-being. I started writing this book just as the clouds of the global Covid-19 pandemic were gathering. In my own corner of the world, amid the ensuing fear and confusion, birds quickly became a source of comfort and escape to millions who – trapped at home and unable to work, travel or visit loved ones – began peering into the sky on their socially distanced walks or listening to the voices that filled the new silence. To many, these delights were a revelation. The challenge now is not to forget; to turn this newfound awareness into action that shores up the future of birdlife around the planet. Birds need us. And, what's more, we need them.

Shoebill

Balaeniceps rex

John Gould was most impressed when, in 1851, a shoebill landed – so to speak – on his desk. 'The most extraordinary bird I have seen for many years', said the celebrated Victorian naturalist, describing the species to the Zoological Society of London. The specimen had been obtained the previous year by German explorer Ferdinand Werne, while traversing the vast Sudd swamps in search of the source of the Nile. It was the first known to Western science.

A veteran of bird-collecting, Gould was not one for hyperbole. Yet the colourful scientific name he gave this species – *Balaeniceps rex* means 'king whale-head' – attests to its impact on him. Today some still call the bird the 'whale-headed stork'. However, its better-known common name, shoebill, derives from the Arabic *abu markub* – 'father of the shoe'. This both celebrates the bird's most prominent feature and is evidence that other cultures knew about the species much earlier. Indeed, the shoebill is identifiable in petroglyphs from the Oued Djerat, eastern Algeria, that date to the early Holocene, when wetlands covered what is now the Sahara.

The taxonomy of the shoebill continues to puzzle scientists today. Gould's initial theory that it was related to pelicans was dismissed; some scientists placed the bird among the herons and others among the storks. But DNA evidence has now returned it to the Pelecaniformes, thus vindicating the celebrated Victorian.

Whatever its name and evolutionary affinities, the shoebill is certainly an imposing creature, standing up to 1.5 metres (5 ft) tall and spanning as much as 2.5 metres (just over 8 ft) across its broad wings. But what Gould found most 'extraordinary' is the enormous beak. Measuring 23 centimetres long by 10 centimetres wide (9 by 4 in), this appendage protrudes like a Dutch clog and is just as capacious. What's more, it comes with a wicked hook on the tip, and sharp slicing edges along the lower mandible.

The shoebill's celebrated beak makes it Africa's ultimate ambush fisher. Standing stock-still in the hidden channel of a papyrus swamp, it lunges at any suitable victim within range, using its bill to scoop, stab and crush all in one. Although its preferred prey is fish such as the African lungfish, it may also target turtles, snakes, water birds and even young crocodiles. Anything that fits the bill, as it were.

That such a distinctive bird managed to elude Western science until 1851 reflects its choice of habitat: the shoebill is confined to some of Africa's most inaccessible wetlands and requires at least 2 square kilometres (¾ sq. mile) of undisturbed territory in which to breed. Although the Sudd, now in southern Sudan, still holds the largest population, Uganda offers the easiest sightings, notably along the Victoria Nile, in Murchison Falls National Park, and around the northern shores of Lake Victoria.

Today the shoebill's range spans nine countries across central Africa, from Sudan in the north to Zambia in the south. With its fragmented population estimated at no more than 8,000 birds, and threatened by swamp drainage, the species is listed by the IUCN as Vulnerable. For birdwatchers worldwide, it remains one of the planet's most sought-after 'ticks'.

Yellow-billed Oxpecker

Buphagus africanus

The annual migration of wildebeest, zebra and other grazers across Tanzania's Serengeti is celebrated as 'the greatest wildlife show on Earth'. For the likes of lions, this immense biomass is dinner. But smaller creatures also find sustenance among the herds – not least this unusual bird, whose entire life cycle depends on them.

Oxpeckers make up the family Buphagidae, which is endemic to Africa. The yellow-billed is one of two species, with – as its name suggests – bill colour being the best means of distinguishing it from its cousin, the red-billed oxpecker (*B. erythrorynchus*). Both are brown, starling-sized birds, invariably seen perched on large mammals. Here they find not only food, but also a platform for preening, roosting and mating, and even hair to line their nests.

The yellow-billed oxpecker occurs in scattered locations across east, west and central Africa. It tends to prefer larger mammals, such as buffalo, wildebeest and domestic cattle, while the red-billed seeks out smaller species such as impala. But both use a variety of hosts, and in regions where their ranges overlap, the two may even line up on the same animal, the yellow-billed generally being dominant.

Naturalists once saw the relationship between oxpeckers and their hosts as textbook mutualism. Large mammals in African grasslands are infested with parasites, such as ticks and botfly larvae. These offer plentiful food to oxpeckers, which swarm over their hosts, probing every orifice and deftly scissoring out the parasites. The deal would thus appear to be win–win: the birds get a free meal; the host gets a personal grooming service. And that service is highly efficient: in one day, an adult yellow-billed oxpecker may take more than 100 engorged ticks or 13,000 larvae.

Today, however, scientists suspect this arrangement to be more one-sided. Close scrutiny reveals that oxpeckers devote much of their attention to their host's wounds and scratches, their pecking and probing serving to keep them open. It transpires that a key component of the birds' diet is blood; many of the ticks they remove have already gorged on it, which is what makes them so tasty. Oxpeckers also pick out earwax and dead skin, thus making as much of a meal of their host as of the parasites it carries. Perhaps, then, it is the birds that are the true parasites.

Research has been inconclusive. One study in Zimbabwe of domestic cattle found that those exposed to oxpeckers lost no more ticks than those that weren't, and also that their wounds took longer to heal. Another conducted on impala, however, suggested that individuals attended by oxpeckers groomed themselves less often than those that weren't. Either way, most host mammals tend to tolerate the discomfort – with the exception of elephants, which swat the birds away with an irritated trunk.

Yellow-billed oxpeckers leave their hosts only in order to breed. They nest during the rainy season, typically in tree cavities, which they line with grasses and hair plucked from their hosts. A female lays two or three eggs, and young birds from a previous brood will help their parents to feed the chicks. After fledging, the youngsters continue to beg for food, even while riding on the backs of their big, hairy new hosts.

Greater Honeyguide

Indicator indicator

An early morning in the dense miombo woodlands of Kafue, central Zambia, finds two men following a bird through the bush. The bird is nothing special to look at – a typical 'little brown job', with a short pink bill and black bib, it might escape most people's notice – but these men, from the local village, know better.

Besides, the bird is clearly inviting the men's attention, twittering persistently as it hops from tree to tree, and flashing its conspicuous white outer tail feathers. Each time they approach, it leads them a little further, its twittering rising to a frenzy when they appear to take a wrong turn. After a kilometre (½ mile) or so, they reach a large baobab, whereupon the bird flits on to an upper limb of the tree and falls silent. It has performed its part of the deal; now its followers must complete theirs.

This avian Pied Piper is a greater honeyguide, and it does exactly what its name suggests: guides people to honey. Sure enough, the men can now hear the telltale hum of a bee's nest emanating from a hole in the trunk of the baobab. Using a smoking branch, they subdue the irate bees before clambering up to scoop out the honeycomb. The bird waits patiently. Once the men have left, it will tuck into the leftovers. This is a time-honoured arrangement, and one that has traditionally provided sticky sustenance to many rural communities across Africa.

Of the 17 species of honeyguide (family Indicatoridae), this species – which occurs in open woodland across much of sub-Saharan Africa – is one of only two known to perform the family's eponymous trick. It is also said to provide the same service for the honey badger, a voracious carnivore with an appetite for honey and a skin thick enough to protect it from stings, although this relationship remains unsubstantiated. Either way, the bird certainly earns its scientific name: *Indicator indicator*.

The honeyguide itself does not eat the honey. Its interest is in the juicy grubs left in the honeycomb – and in the beeswax, which it has a unique ability to digest. When no mammalian help is available, it will go it alone, entering hives early in the morning, when the bees are still torpid, or feeding on nests already ransacked by honey badgers. At times, it may also capture swarming termites and other flying insects.

Convincing large mammals to provide its meals is not the only way in which the greater honeyguide outsources its labour. Like the cuckoo (see page 54), it is a brood parasite, laying its eggs in the nests of other birds – primarily hole-nesters such as barbets and kingfishers – who rear its chicks as their own. The female deposits a single egg in each of several nests, laying up to 20 in a season. She may crush the host's eggs in the process. If not, her young hatchling, still blind and featherless, uses a sharp spur on its bill to puncture the host's eggs and kill its chicks.

There is one caveat for those who wish to exploit the honeyguide's services. African folklore warns that you should *always* leave behind a gift of honey. Otherwise, next time the disgruntled bird will lead you to something less appealing: a black mamba, perhaps, or an angry leopard. You have been warned.

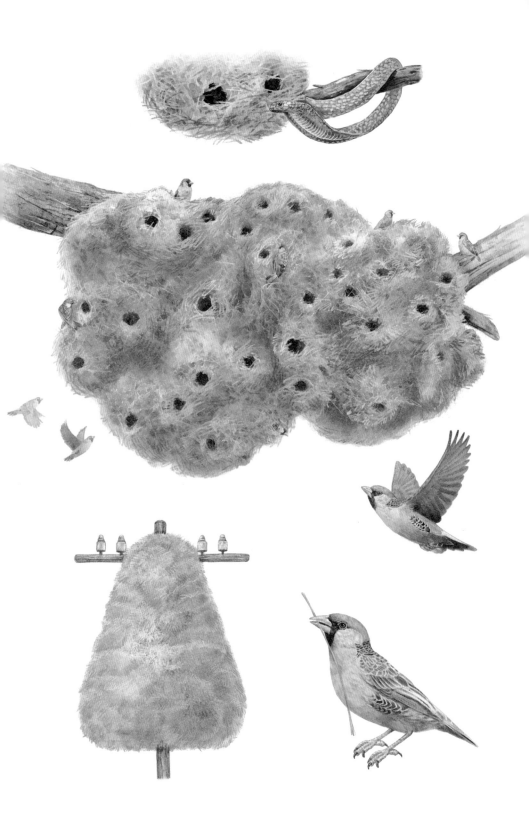

Sociable Weaver

Philetairus socius

Travel the arid landscapes of eastern and central Namibia and you'll soon come across what appear to be giant haystacks stuffed into acacia trees, or even suspended improbably from telegraph poles. These bizarre edifices are the work of the sociable weaver – a small, seed-eating member of the finch family, whose enormous communal nests are among the biggest in the bird world. A large one may measure 5 metres (16½ ft) across and weigh more than a tonne.

Like many weaver birds, sociable weavers nest in colonies. Unlike other species, however, they do not build one nest per pair but instead work together to create a thatched apartment complex that can accommodate over 300 birds in up to 100 individual chambers. One such structure may last for more than a century, housing multiple generations.

Construction typically starts with a platform of strong twigs in the fork of a large tree, such as a camelthorn (*Acacia erioloba*), the velvety pods of which litter Namibia's dry river valleys. The birds then add stiff grass stalks to build up the mass, simply pushing them into the structure, which hangs together from sheer weight. Below, the nest is honeycombed by downward-opening entrance tunnels, each leading to a small nesting chamber, which the birds line with fur, plant fluff or other soft material. Spiky grass stalks stuck into the tunnel walls help to repel intruders such as snakes – notably cape cobras and boomslangs, which seek out unguarded nestlings.

The sociable weaver is endemic to southern Africa, where it inhabits the semi-desert of the Kalahari, ranging from Namibia into neighbouring Botswana and South Africa. It prefers short-grass savannahs, which are less prone to fire than longer grasses. This harsh environment is characterized by its blisteringly hot summer days and cold winter nights, and the dense insulating thatch of the nest serves to shield the birds from the extremes of both.

A nest's residents seldom venture more than a kilometre (½ mile) from home. And they never stop building. The nest remains their home until they die – or, as sometimes happens, it crashes to the ground. Other small birds, including lovebirds, often take over vacant chambers, while larger birds, such as owls, may roost on the roof. One notable tenant is the pygmy falcon: this fierce, diminutive predator helps provide protection for the colony but may also snatch the odd fledgling for its services.

Purple-crested Turaco

Tauraco porphyreolophus

Every September the tiny southern African kingdom of Eswatini downs tools as thousands of girls gather on Ludzidzini royal parade ground to perform the traditional *Umhlanga*, or reed dance. Amid the kaleidoscopic pageantry, one colour is especially vivid: the bright scarlet of the feather headdresses that adorn the king and his royal family. These feathers come from the purple-crested turaco – or, in siSwati, *Ligwalagwala* – a bird long revered in the kingdom for its royal status.

The honour comes at a price for the turaco, which is still captured in numbers to provide for Eswatini's considerable royal population. Sobhuza, father of the present king, Mswati III, is reputed to have had over 500 children. Today, many thousands can thus claim royal descent – and each needs enough feathers for the royal barnet.

The purple-crested turaco is a long-tailed, crow-sized bird, and those royal scarlet plumes are its primary flight feathers. On the living bird, which tends to skulk in dense foliage, they are hard to see until it spreads its wings in short, lurching flights from tree to tree. However, this spectacular creature has colour to spare, with a rich green, purple and rose-pink body set off by a bushy violet crest. These colours are unique in their chemistry: the scarlet comes from a pigment called turacin and the green from one called turacoverdin, both found only in the turaco family.

Turacos belong alongside go-away birds and plantain-eaters in the Musophagidae family, which is endemic to Africa. All are forest-dwelling fruit-eaters, characterized by their bright colours, long tails and rather clumsy manner of flying. Indeed, turacos tend to leap and bound through the branches, taking flight only when pressed – usually starting with a downward glide, then propelled back upwards by a burst of frantic flapping. Scientists have speculated that this form of locomotion may resemble that of the earliest feathered theropod dinosaurs from which birds evolved.

The purple-crested turaco is reasonably common in Eswatini (until recently called Swaziland) and neighbouring areas of northeastern South Africa, and ranges north through eastern Africa as far as southern Kenya. A shy bird, it frequents evergreen forest and woodland, and enters savannah along ribbons of riverine forest, especially where sycamore fig trees provide a plentiful supply of fruit, which it swallows whole. Although a good view

is elusive, its loud, grating *kok kok kok* call is a telltale soundtrack to these habitats.

Royal admiration apart, this bird's spectacular colours are best appreciated by others of its own kind – especially when a male spreads its wings, and puffs up its crest in a pouting breeding display. Once mated, a pair build their platform nest high in a tree, the female laying two or three glossy white eggs. The youngsters leave the nest at just three weeks, using vestigial claws on their wings to clamber around until, 38 days after hatching, they are finally ready to fly.

Bateleur Eagle

Terathopius ecaudatus

In 1889, during an expedition into southern Africa's uncharted interior, a German hunter named Willi Posselt stumbled upon the massive stone walls of an ancient ruined city. In a high enclosure, he found eight carved soapstone figurines, each depicting the same mystical raptor-like bird. Arranged on columns around what looked like an altar, the birds varied in size, with the largest being about 40 centimetres (16 in) tall. Ignoring the pleas of his local guides, Posselt set about plundering what he could.

Today we know these ruins as Great Zimbabwe. Built by the ancestors of today's Shona peoples, the city flourished for some 300 years after its construction in the eleventh century. During colonial times, the Rhodesians would not accept that pre-colonial Africans might have produced a civilization of such sophistication, even suggesting that the city might be the work of the Phoenicians. At Zimbabwe's independence in 1980, however, the new leaders reclaimed their heritage, naming the liberated nation after its famous ruins and placing the bird at the centre of the national flag.

Historians now believe the Zimbabwe bird to have been modelled on the bateleur eagle. This charismatic species has long enjoyed totemic status in the region, revered by the Shona peoples as a messenger from the god Mwari, and thus seems a more likely candidate than the African fish eagle (also proposed as inspiration). The significance of the eight figures has been interpreted in various ways, one being that each represented a king. There is nothing like them anywhere else.

The real bird is just as impressive as it soars above the African savannah. Its common name is often said to derive from the French for tightrope walker – a description of its telltale rocking flight action. In fact, a more accurate translation of *bateleur* is 'street entertainer'. Whatever the case, this medium-large eagle is quickly distinguished from similar-sized raptors by its long-winged, short-tailed flight profile. It glides with minimal effort at low speed and low altitude, spending most of the day airborne and covering more than 500 kilometres (300 miles) as it scans the ground for prey.

By eagle standards, an adult bateleur is unusually colourful, its harlequin plumage of black, pale grey and rufous set off by vivid red legs and face. The large, owl-like head reveals its affinities with the *Circaetus* snake eagles, and it is indeed an expert hunter of reptiles. Birds and small mammals also make the menu – as does carrion, the eagle often appearing at a carcass before the vultures arrive. Bateleurs are reputedly adept at finding a treed leopard kill, and safari guides will sometimes locate the big cat among the branches by first spotting the eagle perched nearby.

Bateleurs frequent open habitats across sub-Saharan Africa, from Senegal southwards to northern South Africa. Pairs form lifelong bonds, reinforced each breeding season through spectacular aerial displays in which the male performs barrel rolls and dives down upon his partner, who rolls on her back to present her talons. The two build their large stick nest in a tree fork. The single youngster may take eight years to shed its brown immature plumage before donning the distinctive garb of adulthood.

And the carvings? During colonial times, the plundered artefacts were scattered far and wide. Several ended up in South Africa – one, famously, at Groote Schuur, Cecil Rhodes's house in the Cape. Most have since been retrieved, and today you can see them in the museum at Great Zimbabwe, now a UNESCO World Heritage Site. Meanwhile their image is ubiquitous in Zimbabwe, from coat of arms to banknotes. Conservationists – worried about the species' recent decline – hope the bird itself shows similar staying power.

Palm-nut Vulture

Gypohierax angolensis

Death, carcasses and carnage are the stock-in-trade of vultures, surely the most confirmed carnivores of the bird world. With a meat-hook bill and eyesight that can clock a kill from 3 kilometres (2 miles) away, these birds are unlikely to opt for the vegetarian alternative. You'd as soon offer lettuce to a leopard.

Nature loves an exception, however, and among Africa's 11 species of vulture, one has evolved to do things differently. The palm-nut vulture is, like the giant panda (*Ailuropoda melanoleuca*), that curious oxymoron of nature: a vegetarian carnivore. The smallest of Africa's vultures, this species eschews the pleasures of the flesh in favour of palm nuts – specifically, the tough nut of the raffia palm. It uses its bill to pull the prize from the tree, often hanging upside-down in the process, then, clutching it in its talons, tears off the tough husk and devours the tasty bit.

In adult palm-nut vultures, some 70 per cent of the diet consists of palm fruit, with the proportion rising to around 90 per cent in juveniles. Even vegetarians have their lapses, however, and this species will sometimes confirm its raptor heritage by snatching dead fish – and the occasional live one – from the shore. It has also been known to eat small mammals, baby turtles, crabs, locusts and even the odd chicken. In The Gambia, this bird is a common sight as it scavenges for leftovers around fishing villages and tourist spots. Elsewhere, it ranges widely across sub-Saharan Africa, though is less common further south, restricted to a select few coastal regions with stands of raffia or oil palms.

Wherever it occurs, this striking and conspicuous bird is quickly distinguished from the African fish eagle (*Haliaeetus vocifer*), whose wetland terrain it often shares, by the greater proportion of white in its plumage – notably in its wings. In flight, it is also more acrobatic than its larger vulture cousins, especially during the breeding season, when pairs may perform rolling, diving aerial displays.

Palm-nut vultures generally nest high in a palm, baobab or euphorbia tree, lining their large stick platform with grass, sisal fibre and dung. Both sexes incubate the single egg, which hatches after four to six weeks. The youngster fledges 85–90 days later but takes at least three years to reach full adult plumage – during which it perfects the skill of cracking the palm nut, preparing for life as a vegetarian vulture.

White-necked Picathartes

Picathartes gymnocephalus

Classical linguists first learning of a bird named 'picathartes' may be intrigued to know what it looks like. After all, a combination of magpie and vulture – which is what *pica* and *cathartes* mean in Latin, respectively – is not easy to visualize. It's true: the species does have a bald head, like a vulture, and a longish tail, like a magpie. However, a decent view reveals that it resembles neither – nor, really, *any* other bird. This may explain why the species so fascinates ornithologists and has acquired such traditional significance in Sierra Leone, one of the countries where it makes its home.

Also known as white-necked rockfowl, this anomalous bird has puzzled scientists since it was first described in 1825 by the Dutch zoologist Coenraad Jacob Temminck. Although variously classified among the crows, starlings and other families, it is now known to be one of just two species in the family Picathartidae – the other being the similar grey-necked picathartes (*P. oreas*), found further east. Taxonomists believe the two are related to the rockjumpers (family Chaetopidae) of southern Africa and the rail-babbler (Eupetidae) of South East Asia, and that the three families collectively represent all that remains of an ancient order that originated in Australia.

The white-necked picathartes is roughly crow-sized, with black-grey upperparts, white underparts and a naked yellow head that sports a large black disc behind each eye. Long-tailed and long-legged, it bounds around the dense undergrowth and rocky slopes of its rainforest home, using its robust, crow-like bill to capture insects and other small creatures on the forest floor. *Dorylus* army ants are a particular favourite, and it will join feeding parties of other forest birds to plunder their columns.

The range of this species extends patchily across western Africa, from Guinea in the west to Ghana in the east, where it was rediscovered in 2003 after having long been thought extinct. It inhabits both primary and secondary rainforest, preferring rocky country, typically around forest inselbergs, where small colonies nest under hidden overhangs. In Sierra Leone, where the largest population occurs, such rocky formations were traditionally believed to house ancestral spirits, and the charismatic picathartes – so closely associated with these places – acquired a totemic status as their guardian. To this day, it commands some residual respect.

Breeding typically takes place in small colonies of up to half a dozen pairs. They live near streams, where the birds find the wet mud required to fashion their deep cup nests beneath a rocky overhang. Pairs are monogamous, raising an average of two chicks in two broods a year. Youngsters fledge some 23–27 days after hatching, gliding down to the ground, where their parents await them with food. Adults are largely silent, although they sometimes utter a chicken-like clucking.

Today the white-necked picathartes is listed as Vulnerable, since fewer than 10,000 are thought to remain. Now an emblem for conservation across its range – including in Gola Rainforest National Park, Sierra Leone – the threats it faces include habitat loss, hunting and collection for the pet trade. The last of these has a certain irony, since it was an expedition to capture these birds for the BBC documentary series *Zoo Quest* in 1954 that first propelled on to our screens one David Attenborough.

KENYA

Lesser Flamingo

Phoeniconaias minor

Your first, distant glimpse of Kenya's Lake Nakuru reveals a bizarre pink wash tinting the shoreline. So lurid is this colour, splashed between the earthy tones of the surrounding savannah and the blue of the mirrored sky at the lake's centre, that it seems to be something synthetic: a slick of candyfloss perhaps, or some hideous chemical effluent. Surely, you think, this can't be birds.

Binoculars reveal the truth: flamingos. Countless thousands of these rose-tinted water birds are crammed into every contour of the lake shore, massing in the shallows, upending in the deeps and commuting over the water in gangly squadrons. Each individual steps out on long legs, head submerged and neck swinging back and forth as it filters food methodically from the surface waters. Further out, displaying birds appear to be travelling on submerged conveyor belts, heads bobbing in comic unison as they move in choreographed conga lines.

Taking flight, the birds appear almost ludicrous, their long necks and legs craning out from a dumpy body, with wings an apparent afterthought. Yet each flock wheels over the water with a collective grace, scattering its elegant reflections across the limpid surface. Small wonder that the whole breathtaking spectacle is one of East Africa's top tourist attractions – the avian equivalent of the Serengeti's 'great migration'.

Blood-red bills identify the great majority of Nakuru's flamingos as lesser flamingos. This species is the smallest and most numerous of the world's flamingos, and distinguished from the greater flamingo – of which smaller groups are visible in the deeper water – by its smaller size, shorter neck and deeper red bill.

Lesser flamingos feed exclusively in alkaline waters, hence their attraction to Lake Nakuru. This is one of a string of East African lakes formed about 25 million years ago during the birth of East Africa's Great Rift Valley, many of which are fed by volcanic springs and known as 'soda lakes'. Today their waters are a soup of aquatic plankton, notably the blue-green algae *Spirulina platensis* on which the lesser flamingo depends and which supplies the carotenoid pigments that keep its plumage pink.

Flamingos are unique among birds in that they feed by inverting their heads and wielding their boomerang-shaped bills upside down. Their food is gleaned through a technique similar to that used by the great baleen whales.

Water is sucked in at the bill's tip and sieved through hairy structures lining the mandibles, known as lamellae, which keep out larger particles of mud. Inside the bill, the bird's large tongue picks the food items from the muddy soup and expels excess water. A small pouch below the bill works like a pump, providing the pressure that powers the whole process.

Lesser flamingo numbers fluctuate from lake to lake as conditions change; if they are not at Nakuru, they might be on Lake Bogoria or Magadi. It is only further south at Tanzania's Lake Natron, however, that they breed. There, more than 2 million pairs – over half the world's population – raise their conical nest mounds of mud and soda slush above waters so caustic that they would strip the flesh from the legs of most birds. After leaving the nest, the ash-grey chicks form dense crèches that may trek tens of kilometres across the salt flats in search of fresh water. Amid such searing heat and scalding waters, the family name Phoenicopteridae feels appropriate: these phoenix birds seem to have risen straight from the fiery cauldron of Africa's prehistory.

Various predators, including African fish eagles (*Haliaeetus vocifer*), spotted hyenas and even baboons, pick off stragglers from the flamingo flocks at Nakuru. On their breeding lakes, the birds have little to fear from other animals. However, the ever-present threat of industrial projects such as soda ash plants explains why, despite its numbers, the IUCN continues to list the lesser flamingo as Near Threatened.

BOTSWANA

Common Ostrich

Struthio camelus

The ostrich needs little description: with males towering up to 2.8 metres (9 ft) tall and weighing over 140 kilograms (300 lb), this is by far the largest bird on the planet. Nowhere is its stature more impressive than against the flat emptiness of Botswana's Kalahari Desert – especially when groups break into a run, raising plumes of dust along the shimmering horizon.

In 2014 one ostrich species became two when DNA studies proved that the Somali ostrich (*S. molybdophanes*), a blue-necked race found only in the Horn of Africa, is genetically distinct. All ostriches found elsewhere – in the Sahel, East Africa and southern Africa – are now classified as 'common ostrich'. Both species belong in the order Struthioniformes, alongside kiwis, rheas, emus and cassowaries. They share with these flightless cousins key adaptations to life on terra firma, including a flat sternum, lacking the keel that anchors flight muscles in flying birds, and soft feathers, lacking the stiff quills to provide the air resistance that gets other birds airborne.

Instead of flying, an ostrich runs. Taking 4-metre (13 ft) strides on its enormous, powerful legs, this bird can reach speeds of 70 kph (nearly 45 mph), making it the world's fastest two-legged animal. Indeed, it can run faster than many birds can fly, using its wings to help it brake and turn. Each foot is balanced on just two toes, with the larger, inner toe sporting a hoof-like nail. These can also deal lethal kicks to predators such as cheetahs; kicks from captive birds on ostrich farms have caused human fatalities.

A male ostrich is larger than a female and has black-and-white rather than grey-brown plumage. During the breeding season he uses an elaborate courtship dance to round up a small harem of mates, sweeping his wings across the ground while proclaiming his territory with a low booming call. The females collectively lay up to 30 eggs in their shallow scrape of a nest. Each weighs more than 1 kilogram (2 lb) and has the capacity of at least 25 hen's eggs – although an ostrich has the smallest egg of any bird in relation to its body size. Incubation rotates between the male at night and the better-camouflaged female by day. The chicks, striped for camouflage, gather in large crèches, presided over by one or two adult birds. Despite such care, only 15 per cent survive their first year.

Ostriches are birds of open and, often, semi-arid country, avoiding well-watered or montane regions. The Kalahari is classic habitat, and although its pickings may appear lean, these birds are versatile feeders, subsisting on a wide variety of plant matter as well as some insects, and able to go for days without drinking. They regularly swallow small stones, known as gastroliths, to help grind food in the gizzard.

It is probably the ostrich's habit of lying down with neck outstretched along the ground, in order to escape detection, that explains the head-in-the-sand myth – an idea supported in the writings of the Roman author Pliny the Elder. In fact, the sheer oddness of ostriches has inspired human culture for thousands of years, from the art of ancient Egypt to Disney's celebrated *Fantasia*. Modern times have seen them farmed as livestock, first for the feather duster trade, which boomed in the early twentieth century, and more recently for the meat and leather industry, which flourishes in such apparently unlikely places as Russia and Alaska. Ostrich egg shells have also long been popular as ornaments, often carved into elaborate forms.

For the San people of the Kalahari, ostriches have never meant commercial profit. Rather, this traditional hunter-gatherer society has long valued the bird as a survival resource, its air-dried flesh providing lasting protein and its eggs, blown of their contents, making perfect water-holders when stoppered and buried in the sand.

Cape Sugarbird

Promerops cafer

The cape sugarbird is a uniquely South African species. With its twittering song and long, flowing tail, this charismatic character cuts an unmistakable dash among the flowering hillsides of the Eastern and Western Cape. Indeed, so closely does it embody the landscape of this southernmost corner of Africa that it could make a fair claim to national bird status, had that honour not already fallen to the blue crane (*Anthropoides paradiseus*). As consolation, it can bask in the reflected glory of the king protea or king sugarbush (*Protea cynaroides*), South Africa's national flower, whose blooms would not appear without its tender ministrations.

Sugarbird and sugarbush are both endemic to the Cape Floral Kingdom, the smallest and proportionally richest of the world's six floral kingdoms, home to over 6,200 endemic plant species. Their home is the *fynbos*, the heathland habitat that dominates this kingdom and comprises numerous families of fine-leaved plants, including the proteas, all of which depend on fire for their ecology. Here, bird and flower have evolved together in symbiotic liaison. The cape sugarbird feeds on the nectar of the proteas, using its fine, curved bill to probe the pincushion-like flower heads and the brush-like tip of its tongue to absorb the sweet liquid. The proteas, in turn, deposit a dusting of pollen on the forehead of the bird, which it transports from bloom to bloom, thus pollinating the plants and propagating the species.

This species is the larger of two in the family Promeropidae, both confined to South Africa. A closer look reveals a streaky grey-brown, sparrow-sized bird with a yellow throat, delicate, curved bill and pale eyebrow. The male's flowing tail, much longer than the female's, may be more than twice as long as his body, giving him an overall length of up to 44 centimetres (17 in).

Sugarbirds are best admired during the breeding season, when the males flit from bush to bush, twittering and flaunting their tails in conspicuous displays that aim both to attract mates and to repel territorial rivals. This takes place in winter, from May to August, which is when rain falls on the Cape, bringing proteas and most other *fynbos* species into flower. Pairs build an untidy cup nest of twigs, pine needles and rootlets, typically in the fork of a protea bush, which they line with protea down. The female lays two eggs, and both parents feed the youngsters when they hatch, providing small insects and spiders collected around the nearby flower heads.

The cape sugarbird is not rare, and is often seen in popular Cape tourist spots such as Kirstenbosch National Botanical Garden. Natural predators such as the cape grey mongoose (*Galerella pulverulenta*) and olive house snake (*Lycodonomorphus inornatus*) are a threat to eggs and nestlings. In the long term, however, a greater concern comes at landscape level, with forces such as development and invasive species threatening the entire ecology of the *fynbos*. The fate of this bird – one of eight bird species endemic to the biome – is inseparable from that of the unique floral home in which it has evolved.

Helmet Vanga

Euryceros prevostii

The island of Madagascar is, in evolutionary terms, a world apart. Marooned in the Indian Ocean during the prehistoric break-up of the supercontinent Gondwana 88 million years ago, its fauna and flora subsequently evolved in blissful isolation. Today some 90 per cent of the native species are endemic to the island. This includes at least 100 of the birds, among them the magnificent helmet vanga.

Had Charles Darwin dropped in on Madagascar before he made it to the Galápagos Islands, he might well have found that vangas – rather than the Galápagos finches (family Thraupidae) – provided all the evidence he needed for his theory of natural selection. One of three bird families unique to Madagascar, and loosely related to the helmet-shrikes and shrike-flycatchers of mainland Africa, these birds provide a striking example of adaptive radiation: the evolutionary principle by which a single founding population isolated on an island evolves different forms to fill different ecological niches. On Madagascar, vangas take the place of birds such as woodpeckers, tits and nuthatches, each species having evolved its own bill shape and feeding techniques to exploit food sources in and around tree trunks and foliage.

None of these bills is more striking than the helmet vanga's. This impressive appendage – at 11–12 centimetres (about 4½ in) the second largest in the vanga family – is bright blue, with an arched upper mandible and hooked tip, and enables its owner to capture large insects, spiders and small reptiles in the forest understorey and lower canopy. A decent view of this secretive forest bird, on the rare occasions it reveals itself, shows that it also has dapper plumage, with jet-black head and underparts set off by a rich chestnut back and upper tail, and a striking white eye.

The helmet vanga is confined to moist tropical forest in a small belt of northeastern Madagascar, occurring largely at altitudes of 400–900 metres (1,300–3,000 ft). There it forages largely in the mid-storey, making fluttering sallies to pluck its prey from the foliage, and sometimes joining mixed feeding flocks with other vanga species. Although the bird itself is hard to see, its long, whistled song – descending and accelerating into a trill – betrays its presence during the breeding season.

This species is monogamous. A pair breed in the southern summer, from September to January, constructing their cup nest of mosses and fibres in a tree fork or bird's-nest fern. That spectacular bill is thought to perform some role in a breeding display – if you've got it, then you must surely flaunt it – although this has not been documented. A female lays two or three eggs, which hatch after 15–20 days' incubation and fledge some 17 days later.

Madagascar has lost more than 90 per cent of its native forest since people first arrived there 2,000 years ago. The helmet vanga, like so much of the island's unique wildlife, is under severe threat as its habitat continues to disappear. Today, with only 6,000–15,000 individuals estimated to remain, the species is listed by the IUCN as Endangered.

Common Nightingale

Luscinia megarhynchos

A girl is in the garden picking rosemary when a songbird lands on her hand and passes her a message. '*Les hommes ne valent rien,*' it sings. 'Men are worthless.' This melancholy story is told in the popular French folk song '*Gentil Coquelicot*'. The bird is, of course, a nightingale (*un rossignol*).

This traditional ditty typifies the role of the nightingale in Western culture. The bird's nocturnal melody has inspired some of Europe's greatest poets, from Homer and Virgil to Shakespeare and Keats, and has long been associated with lost love – and celebrated as an embodiment of the romantic muse. France is no exception. 'Laüstic', one of the earliest known French poems, by the medieval poet Marie de France, takes its title from the Breton word for nightingale. It alludes to the tale of Philomela, from Roman poet Ovid's *Metamorphoses*, who, after being raped by her brother-in-law Tereus, king of Thrace, is transformed into the bird and sings her lament eternally.

Certainly, the nightingale's song is impressive: a stream of phrases, both sweet and dissonant, that fluctuates dramatically in pitch and volume. And by singing at night, when most other birds stop, it amplifies its impact on our ears and invokes romantic associations. But the real nightingale is not quite the bird of the poems. For a start, it is only the male that sings – despite nightingales in verse invariably being female. And he does not do it to lament lost love, nor indeed to express any sentiment other than those of territorial aggression and sexual urgency. Once breeding is underway, the nightly serenade dies down – it is an energy-costly strategy, after all – and by mid-June, apart from their croaking calls, the birds fall silent.

Despite the nightingale's celebrity, many people might struggle to recognize the bird itself. This is thanks largely to its retiring habits: nightingales skulk among thick scrub in open woodland, where they forage near the ground for insects and other invertebrates. They seldom show themselves and, when they do, are nothing special to look at: medium-small brown birds, related to chats and robins in the Old World flycatcher family Muscicapidae, their only distinctive feature is a reddish tail.

Also, nightingales are migrants. They arrive on their European breeding grounds only in mid-April, and by September have set off south for Africa, where they winter in a broad band of tropical savannah, from Senegal to Kenya. Little is known about their behaviour at this time, especially since they are silent. Birds from eastern breeding regions follow an easterly migration route down the Nile valley. Those from further west, including France, skirt the Sahara to the west.

In France, nightingales are common and widespread summer visitors. They take up territories in suitable woodland habitat, where their song rings out during the heady days and nights of early summer. In their nest of grass and twigs low down in a thicket, a pair raises four or five youngsters. With an estimated 3.2–7 million pairs, the species is still listed as Least Concern. However, sharp declines in some regions, including the United Kingdom, have prompted worry that the nightingale, in common with many Afro-Palearctic migrants, is vulnerable to habitat loss along its migratory flyways. If the bird *were* inclined to sing laments, that might be a better reason to do so.

Common Swift

Apus apus

In English folklore, the swift was once known as 'Devil bird'. Today this may seem a little melodramatic. Nonetheless, there is something undeniably other-worldly about these birds, which materialize in British skies every May as if by magic, their rakish silhouettes scything overhead in pursuit of aerial plankton, their drawn-out screams as evocative of summer as any nightingale melody. 'Shrapnel-scatter terror,' wrote the poet Ted Hughes, describing the breakneck energy of a feeding party hurtling overhead.

Swifts have always lived alongside people, typically nesting in the crevices of ancient buildings. *Swifts in a Tower*, David and Elizabeth Lack's classic 1956 study of swifts nesting in the tower of the Oxford University Museum, inspired one of the world's longest-running ornithological studies. Among its revelations was the discovery that swift nestlings can slow their metabolism to enter a state of torpor – a rare trick in birds – and thus survive while their parents disappear on overnight foraging trips.

Modern technology such as satellite geolocators has produced further revelations. We have long known that swifts migrate to and from sub-Saharan Africa. Recent data, however, reveals that one individual may travel 200,000 kilometres (more than 124,000 miles) in a year – thus, during a ten-year lifespan, flying the equivalent of three return trips to the Moon. What's more, given that swifts sleep on the wing, descending slowly from a great height through a series of power naps, we now know that a young bird may spend more than 18 months airborne, not landing once until it breeds in its third or fourth year.

Such claims seem mind-boggling. But you need only watch a swift's crescent form dashing through the air to appreciate how it takes flight to greater extremes than other birds. Not only do swifts feed and sleep on the wing, they also drink, bathe, gather nest material and even mate in flight. Indeed, these birds cannot land on the ground and never touch a solid surface other than at the nest. Their scientific name, *Apus apus*, derives from the ancient Greek for 'without feet' – and, although present, these tiny, sharp-clawed appendages serve only as grappling hooks for vertical surfaces.

Swifts are often confused with swallows (see page 52). The two birds are not related, however. Their similarities in form and lifestyle reflect parallel evolutionary adaptations to the shared challenge of catching flying insects. In fact, swifts are most closely related to hummingbirds, with which they share a common ancestor. The common swift is the most widespread of some 100 species worldwide and breeds throughout Europe and Asia. All populations migrate south to winter in sub-Saharan Africa, leaving their breeding grounds as the supply of insects dries up. In Europe they are fleeting summer visitors, arriving in May and departing by late July, once their young have fledged. In Africa they keep wandering, following weather fronts towards rainfall and the food it brings.

Swifts pair for life and produce an annual brood of two or three chicks. Their crevice nest is fashioned from windblown material glued together with saliva. Parents travel great distances to find food, collecting it in food balls – each consisting of hundreds of individual items – which they bring back to their young. After fledging, the youngsters set off for Africa. If they survive their first year, they may live another ten.

Humans and swifts have a complex relationship. Our felling of forests and erecting of buildings has always benefited these birds, which have been nesting in human structures since at least Sumerian times, 7,000 years ago. Today intensive agriculture is reducing their food supplies, and modern buildings offer fewer suitable cavities. But from the towers of Beijing's Forbidden City to those of the University of Oxford, swifts still occupy a niche, literally, in many of our most sacred places.

European Robin

Erithacus rubecula

In 2015 the 'robin redbreast', as this abundant songbird is commonly known, won a popular poll as Britain's unofficial national bird, trouncing the competition with 34 per cent of the vote. It was hardly a surprise; the robin is surely the most widely depicted of UK species, its red breast adorning countless Christmas cards and its confiding behaviour endearing it to generations of householders and gardeners alike.

The bird derives its scientific name *rubecula* from *ruber*, the Latin for 'red'. Closer scrutiny, however, reveals its signature splash of colour to be more a deep orange. Thus, both scientific and vernacular names are, technically, misnomers. This may be explained by the fact that the word 'orange' didn't enter the English language until the mid-sixteenth century, when *naranjas* first arrived from Spain. By then, 'redbreast' was already in popular usage.

Things are complicated today by the use of 'robin' for unrelated species elsewhere – notably the American robin, *Turdus migratorius*, actually a thrush, which was named by homesick early British settlers who pinned a familiar name on the first bird they saw with a red (orange) breast. This confusion even extended to the Walt Disney movie *Mary Poppins*, in which an American robin popped up in the heart of Edwardian London.

In fact, the European robin belongs to the Muscicapidae family, the Old World flycatchers, and is thus related to chats, flycatchers and other insect-eating songbirds. Its range extends across most of Europe, east into Russia and Iran and south to the Mediterranean shores of north Africa. Attempts by colonists to introduce it to Australia and New Zealand – to create an English rural ambience for settlers as part of the 'acclimatization programme' – failed, thankfully for the native ecology.

This is naturally a woodland bird, which uses its large eyes to forage in low light for insects and other invertebrates. Only really in the United Kingdom has it developed a reputation as the gardener's friend, hopping around flower beds and perching photogenically on spade handles. The roots of this behaviour may lie in Britain's wilder past, when robins habitually foraged around wild boar (*Sus scrofa*), pouncing on any insects exposed by the animals' rooting around. Either way, the bird can become extraordinarily tame around people. This extends to its nesting habits: robins frequently build their neat, moss-lined cup nest inside sheds and outhouses. More bizarre locations recorded include old kettles, watering cans, sun hats and even the pocket of a hanging jacket.

Such apparently trusting behaviour explains the great affection for robins in Britain, one that is not widely shared elsewhere. The bird's endearing appearance helps, of course – that rotund little body, perky stance and bold splash of colour – as does the delicate, trickling song, often the first heard in the morning, the last in the evening (robins may sing on after dark where prompted by streetlights) and the only one audible in otherwise silent winter woods, where most species keep quiet until spring.

This affection has helped to generate the mythology behind the robin as an emblem of Christmas. The Christian explanation holds that a robin flew to comfort Christ on the Cross and was stained with his blood, hence the red breast and, by extension, the connection with the time of his birth. However, the tradition really gained traction during Victorian times, when postmen – who wore red uniforms and were known as robins – delivered the first Christmas cards, many of which depicted the bird as bearer of the card. The Christmas card industry has never looked back.

'A robin redbreast in a cage / puts all heaven in a rage,' wrote the eighteenth-century visionary poet William Blake. It is ironic, given the values of comfort and companionship this species embodies, that it is one of the most aggressive songbirds. Those gentle melodies represent a vigorous territorial contest that continues all year and frequently ends in violence. An estimated 10 per cent of adult mortality in robins is attributed to fighting. Indeed, juveniles must wait six months to acquire their red breast, in order to avoid provoking the aggression of adult males before they've learned to take care of themselves.

Barn Swallow

Hirundo rustica

E very summer Austria's Tyrol province jingles with cowbells as farmers drive their cattle up from the valleys to the alpine pastures. This traditional seasonal movement has helped to shape the landscapes of the Alps, creating meadows where once there was forest and, in the process, providing perfect habitat for Austria's national bird. In the pastures, barn swallows dart around the cattle, finding a rich crop of aerial insects drawn to the cow dung, and open space in which to capture them.

The barn swallow is a historical beneficiary of human activity. The clearing of pasture has extended its natural habitats across the northern hemisphere, while farm buildings have afforded ideal nest sites. A migrant from sub-Saharan Africa, its arrival every spring, with its eye-catching iridescent plumage and companionable twittering, has also made it an icon of summer – hence its emblematic status, in Austria and elsewhere.

For scientists, this species has also proved pivotal to our understanding of bird migration. Early scientists, from the ancient Aristotle to Gilbert White in the eighteenth century, had once explained the annual autumn disappearance of migratory birds with such far-fetched theories as their hibernating at the bottom of ponds. It wasn't until 1912, when a barn swallow ringed the previous year in England was retrieved in KwaZulu-Natal, South Africa, that the truth was established beyond doubt.

Barn swallows start their journey south in September. They gather in large numbers, often perching on power lines, as they feed energetically to build up fat reserves. Once the weather is set fair, they head off, some populations flying west around the Sahara, others east down the Nile valley. Many get all the way to South Africa. En route, small groups converge at traditional roosts, often many thousands strong. The spring return is more direct, with the birds hurrying to reach their breeding grounds. Most Austrian birds will be back on their nests by early April.

This is the most widespread of the world's 83 swallow species and breeds right across the northern hemisphere. Like all swallows, it is adapted for catching small insects on the wing, with its aerodynamic shape, wide gape and rudimentary feet, good for little but perching. It inhabits any open country with abundant insect life. Cattle pasture is perfect: not only do cows leave large piles of insect-attracting dung, they also churn up mud for nest-building and don't crop the grass too low for insects to flourish.

A pair of barn swallows may stick together for several years, usually producing two broods each summer. This species has been building its distinctive mud-and-straw nests on human structures since at least ancient Egyptian times, and has thus colonized areas it might not otherwise inhabit – for example, by using log cabins in the Alps.

Today the barn swallow is one of the world's most numerous birds, with a global population of some half a billion. By October, however, when Austria's dairy farmers are leading their cattle back down to the valleys amid all the pageantry of the annual *Almabtrieb* festival, the birds are already winging their way south, towards another continent entirely.

Common Cuckoo

Cuculus canorus

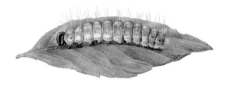

Cu-ckoo, cu-ckoo, cu-ckoo. The two-note chime of the common cuckoo, Europe's least mistakable bird voice, traditionally heralds summer across the continent. It has also provided the bird – and, by extension, its worldwide family, the Cuculidae – with its onomatopoeic name, not only in English and Latin, but also in French (*coucou*), Spanish (*cuco*), Italian (*cuculo*), Dutch (*koekoek*) and German (*Kuckuck*).

It was in Germany, however, that the bird was first immortalized in mechanics. The cuckoo clock, from which a mechanical cuckoo pops out to sound the hour, hails from the Black Forest in the southwest, where it has been manufactured since at least the mid-eighteenth century. Indeed, the first known description, from 1629, was of a clock that belonged to August von Sachsen, Elector of Saxony. The Swiss contribution to this cultural icon did not come until the 1920s, when they added the chalet-style design.

In Germany, as elsewhere in Europe, the cuckoo's strident call is first heard in late April as the birds arrive from their African wintering quarters. This touchstone of seasonal change has long been celebrated in cultures across the continent, from the thirteenth-century Old English poem 'Sumer Is Icumen In', with its joyful line '*Cuccu, cuccu, wel singes þu cuccu*' ('Cuckoo, cuckoo, sing loudly, cuckoo!'), to the musical echo in Beethoven's Pastoral (Sixth) Symphony.

Other cultural associations are less flattering. Cuckoos are brood parasites; in other words, their breeding cycle depends on laying their eggs in other birds' nests and leaving the hosts to rear the young. It is this behaviour that has stamped the bird with the stigma of infidelity, spawning the term 'cuckold' – not that it has any choice in its reproductive strategies.

Despite the loud voice, which falls silent when breeding ends, this is a secretive bird and usually difficult to observe. It is slim and dove-sized, with a long tail and barred underparts, and its resemblance to a sparrowhawk (*Accipiter nisus*) led early scholars to suggest that cuckoos turned into these raptors during winter – although Aristotle wasn't fooled, noting the cuckoo's finer bill. A bird of open or lightly wooded terrain, its insectivorous diet includes a taste for hairy caterpillars that are toxic to other birds.

Only in relatively recent times has science unlocked many of the cuckoo's secrets. We now know that each breeding season, a female will

covertly lay up to 20 eggs, each in the nest of a different host, such as a dunnock (*Prunella modularis*) or reed warbler (*Acrocephalus scirpaceus*). The deception is enhanced by the cuckoo's ability to match its egg colour to that of its host's. Once hatched, the young cuckoo ejects the other eggs or chicks, leaving the adults to rear it as their own. After 14 days, a young cuckoo may be three times the size of its exhausted foster parents.

The youngster never meets its own parents. After fledging, it flies to Africa. Satellite tracking reveals that this species is unusual among Afro-Palearctic migrants in travelling on a broad front, with many birds crossing the Sahara Desert directly. Individuals migrate by night and alone. One bird satellite-tracked from Beijing, China, made a non-stop four-day flight over the Indian Ocean from India to Somalia; it is thought that some individuals may cover more than 16,000 kilometres (9,900 miles) a year.

Whatever its cultural importance, the cuckoo is today in decline across much of Europe, a victim of habitat loss along migration flyways, agricultural intensification and, perhaps, global warming causing its hosts to breed before it can arrive and hijack their nests. For now, it continues to arrive every spring and sound its clarion call for summer, often turning up on the same date year after year. Like clockwork, in fact.

White Stork

Ciconia ciconia

In the spring of 1822 a white stork appeared in the north German town of Klütz. Nothing unusual about that; after all, for centuries these big birds have been welcomed back every year to towns all over Europe. To the astonishment of the townsfolk, however, this individual had an arrow through its neck. Where on earth had it been?

The arrow, it turned out, was of African origin. The bird, now preserved in the University of Rostock, thus provided living proof – decades before ringing allowed scientists to verify bird migration – that when white storks departed every autumn from the German villages in which they'd nested, their destination was thousands of miles away on another continent. Amazingly, another 25 such storks, known in German as *Pfeilstorche*, or 'arrow storks', have since been documented.

Scientists, thankfully, have since found less brutal ways of studying the white stork's migration. This big black-and-white bird, with its predilection for nesting alongside people, has long been celebrated in culture, whether as mythical pilgrim to Mecca or fabled deliverer of babies. That has made its seasonal comings and goings among the easiest of any bird to observe and document. Indeed, this species was the subject of one of the first ever bird-ringing projects, conducted at Germany's Rossitten Bird Observatory from 1906, and in more recent times was among the first birds to be kitted out with satellite transmitters for more precise monitoring.

The nests of white storks are hard to miss. These birds invariably construct their large stick-platform nests on elevated manmade structures, from church towers to telegraph poles. During the breeding season they are very noisy, their bill-clattering greeting displays rattling out like machine-gun fire overhead. A monogamous pair produce up to four chicks each season, and the youngsters, if they can dodge the arrows – or more modern hazards, such as power lines – may go on to live for more than 30 years.

This species breeds across Europe, with concentrations in Iberia, north Africa, Central and Eastern Europe, and western Russia. The great majority overwinter in sub-Saharan Africa, from the Equator to the Cape. They set out from August in large, loose flocks, using thermals to spiral skywards – reaching a height of 1,500 metres (5,000 ft) – then soaring in order to conserve energy. To avoid long ocean crossings, which offer no thermals, they converge on narrow sea straits. Two principal southbound routes have evolved: one westbound, over Gibraltar then around the western fringes of the Sahara; the other eastbound, via the Bosphorus and on down the Nile valley.

In both Europe and Africa, white storks frequent open ground such as marshes, farmland and savannah, where they forage for insects, frogs and other small prey. Historically, human activity has benefited the species, with forest clearance across Europe during the Middle Ages expanding their access to this habitat. In more recent times, industrial development, modern agriculture and uncontrolled hunting along the stork's migration flyways – today with shotguns rather than arrows – have all conspired towards its decline. However, reintroduction projects have returned the bird to former breeding haunts in the Netherlands, Belgium, Switzerland, Sweden and the United Kingdom, and today over 4,000 pairs still return to Germany every year.

Common Raven

Corvus corax

L ate summer in a forest clearing in Karelia, eastern Finland, and the guttural *kronk* of a raven pierces the dawn silence. First one, then two more of these big black birds flap in to alight on a stunted birch, striking gaunt silhouettes in the half-light. Below them, a large brown bear worries at an elk carcass. The ravens have come to claim their share. *Kronk, kronk!* As their calls continue, more of their companions arrive.

Ravens are cemented deeply in many cultures around the world, but nowhere more so than in these northern forests. The name derives from the Old Norse *hrafn*, and Viking chieftains went to war under the raven banner, their god Odin supposedly accompanied everywhere by his raven emissaries Huginn and Muninn. In Finland, legend credits the bird with supernatural powers: shamans kept ravens as pets, and the legendary 'raven stone', a magic egg, supposedly allowed them to learn the mysteries of the ancestors.

The image of ravens as sinister, as reflected everywhere from Shakespeare to horror movies, doubtless stems from the bird's taste for carrion, which once included battlefield corpses. But ravens are also credited with wisdom and prophetic gifts, revered as emissaries between the spiritual and material worlds. To the Haida people of northwestern Canada, for instance, the raven lived in the land of spirits and created the Earth by dropping a pebble in the sea. In Britain, the Tower of London, founded in the eleventh century, will supposedly crumble should its raven mascots ever leave – which explains why the wartime prime minister Winston Churchill imported six captive ravens to replace those lost during the Blitz.

Get beyond the superstition and the common raven is still an impressive bird. All black, with a formidable bill, this buzzard-sized crow is the largest of the world's 6,000 or so species of passerine or 'perching bird'. Its soaring flight can be seen across the northern hemisphere, from boreal forest to rocky desert and Arctic tundra. Its catholic diet includes everything from grains and insects to rodents and carrion. Pairs stick together for life, claiming large breeding territories and reinforcing bonds in aerobatic courtship displays.

The raven's reputation for wisdom is well earned. With one of the largest brains in the bird world, this species demonstrates mental faculties on par with a chimpanzee's (*Pan troglodytes*). These include causal reasoning and an ability to use tools; ravens, for example, will pull up a line from a fishing hole to steal the catch on the end. They also include a prodigious memory, a vocabulary of at least 30 vocalizations, enough self-awareness to both empathize with and manipulate companions, and an apparent capacity to express emotion and enjoy play. Youngsters will creep up behind a large predator in a game of 'catch me if you can', flying away when it turns on them before returning to repeat the process.

Such intelligence and resourcefulness allow ravens to make a living in remote areas where other birds struggle. In northern forests, such as Canada's and Finland's, the birds may even work commensally with wolves (*Canis lupus*), using their carrying calls to alert a pack to a carcass so that the larger predator will open it up and allow all to share.

Common Eider

Somateria mollissima

M ost people – at least, those above a certain age – know what an eiderdown is. The bird from which the product originally derives, however, may be less familiar. The common eider, Europe's largest duck, is a marine species that nests on rocky shores around the North Atlantic. Its long association with people is connected to the miraculous properties of its feathers.

Eider down is, in fact, the layer of soft under-feathers that a female eider duck plucks from her breast to line her nest. It is a remarkable insulator, able to keep eggs and chicks alive in the face of an Arctic blizzard by locking in a layer of warm air when temperatures outside fall as low as -35°C (-31°F). Once widely used to stuff pillows and quilts, it has now largely been replaced by cheaper and less effective synthetic alternatives. A genuine eiderdown is today an extremely expensive luxury item.

Iceland remains one of the few places where eider down is still harvested, notably in the remote Westfjords area, where people have coexisted with the duck since they first settled this remote, sub-Arctic island in the ninth century. Eider down was used as payment by the Vikings and to settle taxes in medieval times. Today Iceland supports some 350 eider farms, which between them produce around 3,000 kilograms (6,600 lb) of eider down a year – most of it going to a wealthy elite in such distant places as Japan and the Middle East.

This small industry is a rare example of the completely sustainable harvesting of a wild natural resource. These are wild birds living wild lives, and unharmed by the collection of their precious feathers. Having spent the winter at sea, they arrive every spring at their colonies, where they nest on the ground, a short walk inland and often among buildings and human artefacts. A nesting female plucks the down from her breast to line her nest – and also to create a brood patch of naked skin through which to transfer her body heat to the clutch of five or six eggs. Only once the 28-day incubation is up and the female has led her brood of hatchlings down to the sea do the farmers move in to collect the down, leaving the nests otherwise intact.

Eider farming passes down through generations in remote coastal communities. When the birds arrive offshore in early spring to pair up – the drakes resplendent in black and white, making their outraged-sounding *ah-ooo!* courtship calls – the farmers strive to attract them on to their nest sites, using fluttering flags, windmills and other lures. Some even play music. Once the ducks are nesting, round-the-clock patrols guard the colony against predators such as gulls and Arctic foxes. Processing the down involves meticulous quality control, first heating it to 120°C (248°F) and then passing it through a series of special traditional cleaning machines. No chemicals are used. The result is a product of extraordinary warmth, softness and lightness; it takes the down from 60–80 nests to produce a single kilogram (2 lb).

It is not only in Iceland that the eider is venerated. This species was the beneficiary of the world's first bird sanctuary, proclaimed by St Cuthbert on the Farne Islands, off the northeast coast of England, in AD 676. Nonetheless, the bird is not universally popular. Its appetite for mussels – which it swallows whole then crushes in its gizzard, ejecting the shattered fragments of shell – has led it into conflict with mussel-farmers, who in some regions have applied to have the bird legally controlled. St Cuthbert would not approve.

Atlantic Puffin

Fratercula arctica

F ew birds are more popular than the puffin. Decked out in dapper tuxedo, with a multicoloured bill and endearing clown's expression, its image appears everywhere from fridge magnet to children's book logo. Nowhere is it more popular than in Iceland, which supports some 60 per cent of the world's population; indeed, in the economics of tourism, the bird is as integral to the island's brand as the Pyramids are to Egypt's.

There is another side to Iceland's relationship with this migratory auk, however. Like many remote islands, its teeming seabird colonies were historically a vital source of food for the inhabitants, who harvested them wholesale. Puffins were highly prized, and today a traditional annual harvest continues, albeit on a greatly reduced scale.

Catching puffins isn't easy. The birds nest in burrows on steep, grassy slopes above perilous sea-cliffs. Traditionally, the puffin-catcher uses the *háfur*, a triangular net on the end of a 6-metre (20 ft) pole, to pluck the puffins from the air as they come in to land. The birds are stripped to their breast muscles, then frozen or salted for sale or consumption. Experienced catchers once took 5,000–6,000 in a season, always sub-adults.

Puffins are present on Iceland – indeed on all their breeding colonies – only during summer. Arriving in April and May, pairs tidy up their burrows, which they either dig themselves or, in some places, appropriate from rabbits, and reaffirm their lifelong bonds with head-wagging courtship displays, standing sentry beside their burrow entrance to deter challengers. The single chick is fed in the burrow by both parents. Their fishing trips may entail overnight commutes to fishing grounds 80 kilometres (50 miles) offshore, returning with dozens of tiny fish (typically sand eels) held in their bill – kept in place by a muscular, grooved tongue while the bird pursues even more.

The puffin chick – known as a puffling – leaves the burrow after six weeks, alone and at night to avoid predators such as gulls. It heads straight out to sea, not returning to its colony for two or three years and not breeding until the age of five. Indeed, all puffins spend the non-breeding months – September to March – at sea, dispersing across the North Atlantic, as far south as the Canary Islands, as they ride the winter storms. They are well adapted to this testing environment, using their webbed feet and paddle-like wings to catch fish deep underwater with the agility of penguins.

Today the Atlantic puffin is in decline. Although some 3–4 million pairs still nest on Iceland, numbers are falling worldwide and in 2015 the IUCN upgraded its conservation status to Vulnerable. This, naturally, has raised concern about Iceland's puffin harvest. Today the practice is carefully controlled, with strict limits and licences, a three-day capture window and only certain areas exploited – mainly in the north, where the largest colonies still thrive. It continues more by tradition than by necessity, since the economic value of puffin tourism now far outstrips that of puffin flesh.

In truth, puffins now face much graver threats than the *háfur*, with depleted fish stocks and warming seas both having a serious impact on the birds' food supply and hence their breeding success. The residents of Heimaey island, off southern Iceland, are doing their bit to help. Every August countless disorientated young birds, befuddled by harbour lights, crash-land as they leave their burrows for the sea. A midnight posse of schoolchildren – the 'puffling patrol' – sets out to rescue them, using flashlights to scoop up the youngsters then gathering the following morning for a ceremonial release into the sea. This popular ritual both celebrates the bird's importance to the island and allows scientists to collect vital data for its conservation.

Little Owl

Athene noctua

O n 28 February 2002, the Greek drachma finally lost its legal status. Greece had joined the Eurozone and the transitional period, during which the euro was introduced, had now come to its official end. One important symbol survived the change, however. The little owl, long emblazoned on the back of the one-drachma coin, simply hopped across to assume its proud position on the back of the Greek one-euro.

The tradition is an ancient one. A silver tetradrachm coin, now preserved at the Museum of Fine Arts in Lyon, France, reveals that the ancient Greeks depicted little owls on their coins as early as 479 BC, after the Battle of Thermopylae. Indeed, in daily use, these Athenian drachmas were called γλαῦκες, which means 'owls' in ancient Greek. This diminutive, nocturnal bird of prey was identified in Greek mythology as sacred companion to Pallas Athene, the goddess of wisdom and patron deity of Athens. Ancient Greek art and iconography was swarming with little owls.

This ancient association is honoured in the bird's scientific name: *Athene noctua* means 'Athene of the night'. History does not record how the bird acquired its sacred status. It is clear, however, that this charismatic owl has always lived cheek-by-jowl with humankind, its distinctive silhouette popping up around farm buildings today just as it did in ancient times. As with all owls, its large head and piercing stare suggest wisdom and perspicacity, while its ability to operate by night suggests supernatural powers, all of which would seem to make it a fitting companion for a goddess. Moreover, the bird's appetite for cockroaches and other pests has long made it welcome around human dwellings.

In Europe, the little owl is the only member of the owl genus *Athene*. Thrush-sized, with striking white eyebrows, it is typically seen perched on walls or buildings, though it is equally at home in rocky semi-deserts – in short, wherever it can find suitable holes for nest sites. It hunts largely at dusk and, like many small owls, punches above its weight, taking anything from beetles to baby rabbits.

In spring, males utter a rising, cat-like courtship call. Pairs mate for life, raising up to five young per year, and habitually perch together. Although locally common, this species is under threat from pesticides, which deplete its supply of insect prey. As with all predators, its ecological value – whether totted up in drachmas or in euros – is incalculable.

Alpine Chough

Pyrrhocorax graculus

Picture a busy lunchtime at a ski resort high in the Swiss Alps. As skiers remove gloves and goggles to grab a sandwich, a chorus of trilling calls announces a posse of birds. Jet-black against the chocolate-box backdrop, they swoop in around the diners, foraging busily for crumbs before lifting up again to alight on the café roof.

These birds are alpine choughs, also known as yellow-billed choughs, from their most colourful feature. Sociable, jackdaw-sized members of the crow family (Corvidae), they are among the world's highest-altitude birds, living among mountain peaks from the Alps to the Himalayas. Nesting has been recorded at 5,500 metres (18,000 ft), higher than any other bird, and climbers have spotted individuals a staggering 8,200 metres (26,900 ft) above sea-level.

Survival at such extremes requires unusual adaptations. Alpine choughs' embryos have special haemoglobin, with an enhanced affinity for storing oxygen, and their hatchlings – unlike the naked chicks of most other songbirds – are covered in a soft insulating down for protection against the cold. The birds are also highly skilled in exploiting mountain air currents, using their broad, heavily fingered wings to fly with great buoyancy and agility.

During the summer breeding season, alpine choughs remain high in the mountains, foraging for insects in the alpine meadows. In winter, they descend to the valleys by day in search of berries and other fruit, returning to the crags only to roost – a daily altitudinal commute of up to 1,600 metres (5,250 ft). However, this seasonal pattern has been skewed in some areas – including the Swiss Alps – by the mushrooming of ski resorts. With a versatility typical of corvids, alpine choughs have been quick to seize on the ready supply of leftovers and handouts, remaining up on the slopes through the late winter months, when the resorts are at their busiest. In the process, they often become very tame.

Alpine choughs pair for life, making their bulky stick nests in rock crevices. Adults forage in small, noisy flocks, often taking off to swirl through the empty airspace over the cliffs and canyons. This species remains reasonably common in appropriate terrain but, like many birds whose natural history is tied to the snow line, it stands to lose ground as climate change erodes its alpine habitat.

Bearded Vulture

Gypaetus barbatus

Crack! A sharp report rings out from a ravine high in the Spanish Pyrenees. You look up to see a large bone clattering over the boulders below, shattering as it tumbles. Seconds later, a shadow sweeps across the cliff face as a huge bird glides down to alight beside the broken pieces. Now you understand. It was the bird that dropped the bone, breaking it quite deliberately, and it's coming to retrieve the spoils.

Quebrantahuesos – literally 'breaker of bones' – is the Spanish name for what English-speaking ornithologists know, more prosaically, as the bearded vulture. This enormous bird of prey is unique among vertebrates in being the only species that feeds almost entirely on bones, which it obtains from animal carcasses found in its mountain lair. To break these bones into more manageable chunks, it has evolved the ingenious technique of carrying them aloft and dropping them to smash into pieces on the rocks below. This trick may take a youngster seven years to perfect.

You might think bones a rather unappetizing, not to say awkward, diet, but the bearded vulture gets up to 90 per cent of its nourishment from this source, and bone marrow is highly nutritious, rich in fat, and remains so for months after the rest of a carcass has rotted away. The bird swallows impressively large chunks whole, its fearsome stomach acids breaking them down in less than 24 hours.

Bearded vultures live at high altitudes – often above 2,000 metres (6,500 ft) – in mountain ranges across Eurasia and Africa, from the Pyrenees to the Himalayas and from the Ethiopian Highlands to South Africa's Drakensberg. Throughout this range, their curious lifestyle has long given rise to myth and superstition. The birds were once heavily persecuted across much of Europe, erroneously blamed for snatching livestock and even children (the bird's alternative name, lammergeier, is German for 'lamb slayer'). In Iran, by contrast, the bird has always been a harbinger of good fortune, and anybody who killed one was traditionally doomed to die within 40 days.

It is from ancient Greece, where prophetic powers were attributed to the bird, that one of the most curious stories hails: the playwright Aeschylus reputedly met an unfortunate demise when an eagle dropped a tortoise on his head. Given that the bearded vulture may sometimes deploy its bone-smashing technique on tortoise shells, historians speculate whether this species might have been the real culprit.

Irrespective of myth and folklore, the bearded vulture is unmistakable. Measuring up to 2.8 metres (9 ft) across its long, narrow wings, it differs from other vultures in having a fully feathered head and neck, including the tufted 'beard' of feathers below the bill from which it gets its English name. Pairs occupy huge territories in remote, rugged terrain, building massive stick nests in which they raise one or two chicks, which sometimes remain dependent on their parents for up to two years.

This unusual raptor is in decline worldwide, and was upgraded by the IUCN in 2014 to Near Threatened. In Europe an ambitious reintroduction programme is working to restore the lost population in the Alps. For now, Spain remains the continent's best location in which to glimpse the breaker of bones, with a population of some 100 breeding pairs that appears to be slowly increasing.

Hoopoe

Upupa epops

On a warm spring day in a Tuscan olive grove, a soft but persistent three-note melody punctuates the drone of the cicadas: *hoo–poo-poo, hoo–poo-poo, hoo–poo-poo* … You needn't be an ornithologist to identify the singer. After all, few birds have a more satisfyingly onomatopoeic name than the hoopoe. In Italy, where this colourful migrant has long been heralded as a harbinger of spring, it is *upupa* – essentially the same, but with a more Mediterranean flourish.

Once spotted on its high perch, this thrush-sized songster is unmistakable. The combination of long, down-curved bill and folded crest gives its head a unique pickaxe profile. Then, when it takes off in a floppy-winged, moth-like flight, it bursts into colour, the warm cinnamon body set off by vivid black-and-white stripes across wings and tail, and the crest flaring into an impressive fan as it alights. A real show-stopper.

An olive grove makes the ideal home for a hoopoe, providing both the open ground on which it can probe for worms, beetles and other tasty titbits, and plentiful cavities among the gnarled tree trunks and tumbledown stone walls in which to construct its nest. In fact, this species has a wide habitat tolerance, occurring from farmland to steppes. And wherever it breeds, autumn sees it heading south to winter quarters along the southern fringe of the Sahara.

The hoopoe's breeding behaviour is perhaps less appealing than its appearance. A female lays her clutch of up to ten eggs deep in the nest cavity, and is fed by the male through a narrow entrance. To deter predators, both parents rub foul-smelling secretions from their uropygial gland – at the base of the tail – into their plumage and around the nest, creating a stink of rotting meat. Additionally, the nestlings hiss like snakes, and can squirt their droppings through the narrow nest hole forcefully and accurately into the face of an intruder. Best to keep your distance.

The combination of memorable call, gorgeous plumage and bizarre behaviour has ensured the hoopoe a prominence in Mediterranean cultures since ancient times. The bird appears in Egyptian hieroglyphics from around 2000 BC, and featured in the mythology of the Minoans and ancient Persians. In the plays of Aristophanes, it was the King of Birds, and in the Torah, it led King Solomon to meet the Queen of Sheba. Indeed, in 2008 Israel honoured the hoopoe by voting it the national bird.

Arctic Tern

Sterna paradisaea

Visitors to the remote Arctic settlement of Longyearbyen in early summer might wonder why residents walk around brandishing sticks. A stroll around the harbour soon provides the answer. Venture too close to the breeding colonies of the Arctic terns, whose shallow nests (known as 'scrapes') are crammed into any available scrap of ground, and the birds take to the air in shrill, screeching outrage, swooping and fluttering around your head, blood-red bills poised to strike.

This feisty threat display aims to deter nest predators such as skuas and Arctic foxes, and is vigorous enough to halt a polar bear in its tracks. Tourists don't stand a chance. Locals, however, have learned that a stick in the air will distract the irate seabirds long enough for its bearer to slip past and out of the danger zone.

Longyearbyen, capital of the Norwegian archipelago of Svalbard, is the northernmost town in the world – just 1,000 kilometres (620 miles) from the North Pole. In mid-June, at peak breeding season, the terns here enjoy 24 hours of sunlight. Remarkably, however, they were experiencing exactly the same thing just a few months earlier, on the opposite side of the globe. This is because, while the Arctic tern breeds in and around the Arctic Circle, its range extending along the northern coastlines of North America, Europe and Asia, it migrates every year to spend the northern winter around the *Antarctic* Circle, thus enjoying the southern summer. This bird never experiences winter; indeed, it probably sees more daylight than any other animal on the planet.

The statistics that this globetrotting lifestyle generates are mind-blowing. A group of Arctic terns satellite-tagged in the Netherlands in 2013 were found to have covered an average distance of 90,000 kilometres (56,000 miles) in a single year – about twice the circumference of the Earth. Indeed, one bird during its lifetime may fly the equivalent of four return trips to the Moon. And the routes it takes are not straightforward. Many birds, having travelled south down the Atlantic, may divert thousands of kilometres east, even to Australia, before heading south to northeastern Antarctica. Like many seabirds, they do not simply follow the shortest route, but must navigate according to such variables as wind and food. This helps to explain why in 1982 a bird ringed in the Farne Islands off northeastern England was retrieved three months later in Melbourne, Australia.

Seen up close at its breeding colonies, the Arctic tern appears a mere slip of a creature: too fragile, you might imagine, to complete such Herculean journeys. Yet this bird is built to travel. Long, slim wings power a buoyant flight, enabling it to spend days aloft, gliding for long periods and even snatching brief naps, while its prowess as a fisher – plunge-diving to grab small fish and marine invertebrates just below the surface – means that it is never short of food en route. Back at their northern breeding colonies, pairs renew their bonds with gifts of fish during an elaborate courtship display. Each female lays two eggs. The chicks fledge 21–24 days after hatching, then must start out with their parents on the epic journey south.

Steller's Sea-eagle

Haliaeetus pelagicus

In 1733 the Great Northern Expedition set sail from Kamchatka, in the far east of Russia, on what was to become one of the greatest ever explorations. Led by the Danish commander Vitus Bering, it was the first to circumnavigate the north Pacific, revealing to Europeans for the first time the existence of Alaska and the Bering Strait. Many of the crew perished, including Bering, but the expedition's pioneering naturalist Georg Steller kept the survivors alive and made it back in the spring of 1743. Today his name is enshrined in the creatures he discovered. Among them is the largest eagle in the world.

Few birds look more impressive than Steller's sea-eagle. With its striking snow-white and chocolate livery, piercing glare and yellow hatchet of a bill, this massive raptor lords it over the wild coastal forests of the Russian far east. Although closely related to America's bald eagle and Eurasia's white-tailed eagle, it exceeds both in size. Indeed, with larger females averaging 7.6 kilograms (17 lb), occasionally pushing 9 kilograms (20 lb), it tops even the formidable harpy eagle of South America (see page 144). In flight, revealing its signature diamond-shaped tail, its wingspan may exceed 2.3 metres (7½ ft).

The breeding range of Steller's sea-eagle extends from the Kamchatka Peninsula around the nearby Russian coast and inland along the lower Amur River. In winter many of these birds travel south, drifting with the sea ice out to Russia's southern Kuril Islands and as far as Hokkaido, Japan. Numbers peak in late February in the Nemuro Strait, where the birds gather beside white-tailed eagles in arguably the world's most spectacular assemblage of large raptors.

Like other sea-eagles in the genus *Haliaeetus*, this huge bird feeds primarily on fish, scanning from a raised perch or while circling over the water, then swooping to pluck its prey from the shallows with a lunge of its fish-hook talons. Salmon and trout are favourite prey, but this versatile predator also takes water birds, and has been known to carry off hares, Arctic foxes and other mammals. As with all sea-eagles, it is not above scavenging – many wintering birds in Japan subsist on deer carcasses – and it will also steal food from other eagles and its own kind.

The breeding season begins in late February with the pair performing soaring display flights. They build their huge stick nest in a large riverside tree or on a rocky costal outcrop, and the female lays one to three eggs that are the biggest on average of any eagle. Usually only one chick survives to adulthood. It remains dependent on its parents for several months and takes five years to acquire full adult plumage.

An adult Steller's sea-eagle has few natural enemies. However, anthropogenic threats including habitat loss, industrial pollution, over-fishing and persecution are of greater concern. Heavy flooding along Russian rivers, attributed to climate change, has caused widespread nesting failure. Today, the IUCN lists the species as Vulnerable, with a world population estimated at fewer than 5,000 individuals.

MONGOLIA

Golden Eagle

Aquila chrysaetos

Many parts of the world claim the golden eagle as their own. Indeed, this iconic raptor is the national emblem of five nations – Albania, Germany, Austria, Mexico and Kazakhstan – and thus arguably the most popular national animal in the world. It was the standard under which the Roman legions marched across Europe – echoed centuries later in the regalia of the Nazis – and is the bird of Tennyson's celebrated 'He clasps the crags with crooked hands' poem.

Mongolia, however, has a better claim than many. Here, in the Altai Mountains, a small community of 'eagle hunters' still practise the ancient art of *berkutchi*: training golden eagles to fly from the gloved wrist to capture foxes and other game. The hunters are of Kazakh descent but fled their homeland during Communist rule to preserve their nomadic lifestyle. Learning to rear these powerful birds starts in childhood and ultimately produces a bond of extraordinary closeness between eagle and trainer. Today some 250 eagle hunters remain. Each October they gather in a festival of rich pageantry, their birds displayed to admirers while, on horseback, they fly them in various challenges against a suitably wild mountain backdrop.

Taming a golden eagle is no picnic. This formidable hunter may weigh 5 kilograms (11 lb) and have a wingspan of more than 2 metres (6½ ft), and its talons grip harder than a Rottweiler's jaws. Stooping at speeds of up to 250 kph (155 mph), it can kill animals as large as roe deer, although typical prey comprises smaller fare such as hares, marmots and grouse. Hunting technique varies from a long attacking glide, the eagle having first spotted its prey while on high, to low quartering of a hillside, snatching prey flushed into the open.

This species is the largest in the *Aquila* genus of 'booted' eagles, named for their feathered tarsi (lower legs). Females are 20–30 per cent bigger than males, but size varies between regional races; the largest is the Himalayan while the smallest is the Japanese. Adults are largely dark brown, with a paler nape that flashes gold in sunlight (hence the name). Immatures have white patches on wings and tail that disappear by the time they acquire adult plumage in their fifth year. When soaring, a golden eagle holds its wings in a signature shallow 'V', the primary feathers splayed like fingers. When gliding or stooping, it sweeps them back, with fingers closed.

83

Few raptors are more widely distributed than this one. It ranges across the northern hemisphere from Iberia through central Asia to the American west. It requires large, undisturbed tracts of open country with cliffs or crags for nest sites. Mountains are not a prerequisite – this eagle also frequents semi-desert, prairie and steppe – but with breeding territories measuring up to 200 square kilometres (77 sq. miles), a pair always needs plentiful space. The huge stick nests are reinforced each year, and grow over time to 2.5 metres (more than 8 ft) across. Generally, only the older of the two chicks survives. It stays with its parents for a few months after fledging, but disperses within a year to find its own range. Youngsters that survive the tricky early years may live to over 30.

Today the IUCN lists the golden eagle as Least Concern, with an estimated 60,000–100,000 breeding pairs worldwide. However, populations have declined steeply since the Industrial Revolution, and continue to do so. Despite the bird's revered status in Mongolia, and its cultural clout worldwide, it remains unpopular in many regions, accused of killing livestock. This accusation is greatly exaggerated; eagles caught feeding on lamb carcasses, for example, are generally scavenging from an animal that was already dead. Retribution – in the form of shooting and poisoning – nonetheless continues. Meanwhile, the more insidious perils of pesticides and habitat destruction ramp up the pressure on this magnificent bird.

Bar-headed Goose

Anser indicus

As sunset shadows lengthen over the forbidding peaks of the high Himalayas, a chorus of honking announces an approaching flock of birds. Emerging from a pass and rising in V-formation over the snowfields, the birds flap resolutely onwards into the falling dusk, charting their northward course over the roof of the world.

Some migrating birds are celebrated for the distance they travel, and others for their speed. The bar-headed goose of central Asia is remarkable for the height it reaches. Altitudes are hard to verify, with anecdotal records of over 8,481 metres (27,824 ft) on Makalu unconfirmed, but in a project by the University of Bangor, Wales, in 2012 that fitted 91 geese with satellite transmitters, one individual was recorded at 7,290 metres (23,917 ft). That's still pretty astonishing for any warm-blooded animal without the benefit of bottled oxygen.

The birds undergo this punishing ordeal in order to reach their breeding grounds. Bar-headed geese breed in central Asia, on the high plateaus of China, Kazakhstan and Mongolia, with Lake Qinghai in western China supporting the most. They spend winter to the south, on the low-lying wetlands of the Indian subcontinent. Travelling between the two involves flying twice a year over the world's highest mountains.

Such altitudes pose significant problems for flying birds. With temperatures far below freezing and the air starved of oxygen, respiration is difficult, and flight muscles must work harder to generate the extra lift required. Bar-headed geese meet this challenge with special adaptations, including larger lungs than similar-sized geese and a higher capacity for carrying haemoglobin in the blood. This helps them to breathe more efficiently and get more oxygen to the flight muscles. They also have a relatively larger wing area, producing extra thrust and lift.

Satellite tracking has shown that bar-headed geese may cross the Himalayas from sea-level in one non-stop flight of as little as seven hours. This entails the greatest rate of continuous climbing recorded in any bird. Flocks follow a 'rollercoaster' flight path, dropping into passes in order to lower their heart rate, then using updraughts to regain height and cross the peaks and ridges. Flying at night, when the air is colder and denser, allows greater lift – and makes it easier to avoid lurking golden eagles.

The bar-headed goose is a handsome silver-grey bird, with a bright-orange bill and two distinctive black bars on its crown. It has featured in the culture of China and southern Asia since ancient times, being a motif of fidelity and inspiring characters in ancient Sanskrit literature. At Lake Qinghai it forms large, loose colonies, sometimes thousands strong. Pairs mate for life. The female lays three to eight eggs in a nest on the ground, while the male helps to deter predators such as crows and foxes. The young leave the nest a few days after hatching, and can fly at 55–60 days.

After recrossing the Himalayas on their southbound migration, bar-headed geese disperse across India, from Assam to Tamil Nadu, and into Bangladesh, many settling on cultivated plains, where they guzzle crops. Today the IUCN lists the species as Least Concern. In Qinghai, it has suffered from outbreaks of bird flu, but the population is estimated at 97,000–118,000 and increasing. It is prized in ornamental wildfowl collections worldwide, and individuals have lived up to 20 years in captivity.

Golden Pheasant

Chrysolophus pictus

An ornate bird perches on the branch of a hibiscus tree amid a confetti of butterflies and blossom. Its dazzling colours are faded now – this bird was painted nearly 1,000 years ago – but its lines remain as exquisite as when the artist first put ink to silk, during the Song Dynasty. The right side of this scroll bears a golden calligraphic inscription in the hand of Emperor Huizong, proclaiming the bird's virtues: its refinement (the crest), its martial prowess (the claws), its bravery (the confronting of rivals), its benevolence (the sharing of food) and its punctuality (the unfailing call at dawn).

The bird is a golden pheasant, and this masterpiece, 'Golden Pheasant Resting on Hibiscus Branch' (*Furing Jinji Tu*), is today preserved in Beijing's Palace Museum. Attributed to a court painter during the reign of Emperor Huizong, it is one of countless images of this dazzling species, which has long enjoyed a rich symbolism in China. During the Song Dynasty (AD 960–1279), women wore robes emblazoned with golden pheasants for state occasions. During the later Ming Dynasty, the bird was a symbol of status and embroidered on a badge worn by civil servants of the second rank. To this day, it gives its name to Chinese restaurants the world over.

The golden pheasant is endemic to the mountainous forests of western China. And, of all China's spectacular pheasants, none is more colourful or ornate. Its species name, *pictus*, 'painted', perfectly describes the male's improbably vivid combination of scarlet body, blue and green wings and golden cape. It might equally, of course, refer to the frequency with which this gorgeous livery has been depicted by painters.

Colours aside, this is a relatively small pheasant, with its tail plumes accounting for more than two thirds of its 1-metre (3 ft) length. Like most gamebirds, it is strongly sexually dimorphic, the smaller female having none of her male's technicolour splendour but instead dressing down in subtle browns for concealment at the nest. These retiring birds are hard to observe, foraging on the ground in dark forests and taking flight only when pressed or when retiring to their treetop evening roosts. During the breeding season, the male calls loudly at dawn and performs impressive cape-flaring courtship dances for females, also using his sharp-clawed feet to battle rival males.

The beauty of the golden pheasant has long made it a popular cage bird. It was the first pheasant brought to America, in 1740, and George Washington reputedly had his own birds at Mount Vernon. Feral populations have since established themselves in many countries, including Canada, Australia, Argentina and the United Kingdom. In captivity, this species may live for more than 15 years, and breeders have created many hybrid strains, notably Lady Amherst's pheasant (*Chrysolophus amherstiae*). It is faring less well in its native home, however, with habitat loss and the pet trade both taking their toll. At present, the IUCN lists its conservation status as Least Concern.

Japanese Crane

Grus japonensis

Few birds are more naturally emblematic than the Japanese crane. Towering up to 1.5 metres (5 ft) tall on its long legs, its snow-white plumage adorned with bold black markings and a fiery-red naked crown, it would be striking enough even if it simply stood still. But, come the breeding season, pairs perform one of the most impressive courtship ballets in the animal kingdom, crouching, stretching and leaping in perfect tandem, all the time filling the frigid air with their wild, bugling cries.

Add to this the qualities of fidelity – the birds mate for life – and longevity – they live up to 40 years in the wild and have reached 75 in captivity – and it is hardly surprising that this species, also known as the red-crowned crane or *tanchōzuru*, is deeply embedded in the culture of Japan. Legend holds that it lives for 1,000 years and brings good fortune to those who make sacrifices. Today its image is emblazoned on everything from chopsticks and kimonos to lift doors and the logo of Japanese Airlines.

More surprising, perhaps, is that just a century ago Japan very nearly allowed this national icon to become extinct. Once widespread across the islands, it was hunted remorselessly in the late nineteenth and early twentieth centuries. By 1924 fewer than 20 birds remained, all confined to the Kushiro marshes on the northern island, Hokkaido. Conservation finally got underway in 1935, when the bird was declared a national monument. With protected land set aside and additional food provided in winter, the population slowly recovered. By 1959 it had reached 150 and early in the twenty-first century it passed the symbolic milestone of 1,000. Today there are approximately 1,300 Japanese cranes in Japan, all on Hokkaido, where the bird was traditionally deified by the Ainu people as Sarurun Kamuy, 'god of the marshes'.

Japan's cranes are resident. They breed in the marshes in spring and move out to the rice fields during Hokkaido's snowy winter, travelling no more than 150 kilometres (90 miles) in the process. However, a small migratory population also inhabits mainland Asia. These birds breed in Siberia, northeastern China and northeastern Mongolia, and migrate in autumn to the Korean Peninsula and north-central China. In Chinese and Korean culture the birds are similarly revered: in Taoist literature, immortals typically ride on them, and tombs from the Shang Dynasty are emblazoned with their image. As in Japan, however, culture has not saved the bird from a dramatic decline over the last century, especially through the loss of its breeding grounds to agriculture.

The Japanese crane is the heaviest of the world's cranes, weighing up to 10.5 kilograms (23 lb). It is a sociable species, foraging on open ground in family groups that band together into larger flocks at roosts and when travelling between feeding grounds. Its food comprises both small aquatic animals, from insects to rodents, and grain – the latter taken mostly in winter, when the birds descend on paddy fields. Adults reach breeding maturity at three to four years and form lifelong monogamous pairs. After the noisy ceremonies of courtship, they construct a nest on open marshy ground. A female usually produces two eggs, and the two partners share in incubating these and rearing the chicks, defending them vigorously from predators such as foxes. The youngsters fledge after 95 days but stay with their parents for nine more months.

Today, 11 of the world's 15 crane species are threatened with extinction, and – with an estimated global population of between 2,800 and 3,430 – the Japanese crane is no exception. As the Asian mainland population continues to decline, however, at least the country that bears the bird's name continues to offer hope for its future.

Northern Mockingbird

Mimus polyglottos

First things first: there is no evidence that this popular suburban songster has ever deliberately mocked anybody. Yes, it has an impressive ability to imitate the voices of others, but not for the purpose of teasing them. Its aim, rather, is to expand its own repertoire in order to impress members of its own species. 'Mimicbird' might be more fitting – and indeed, this is spelled out in the bird's scientific name; *Mimus polyglottus* is a Latin and ancient Greek combination that means 'many-tongued mimic'.

Outside America, the northern mockingbird is best known from songs and stories. In the title of Harper Lee's classic *To Kill a Mockingbird* (1960), the bird is a metaphor for innocence, and in the traditional lullaby 'Hush Little Baby' it represents a gift to a child ('Mama's going to buy you a mockingbird'). This species is also the state bird of Arkansas, Florida, Mississippi, Tennessee and Texas. For a small bird, it makes a big impression. Thomas Jefferson was so taken with it that he kept a pet one named Dick.

This species has among the most complex and intriguing songs of any bird. Up to 203 different song types have been identified, many deriving phrases from other species, such as the Carolina wren (*Thryothorus ludovicianus*) and the northern cardinal (*Cardinalis cardinalis*). It can also imitate cats, dogs and crickets, and make a stab at mechanical noises such as car alarms and squeaky hinges. All these sounds are incorporated into repeated phrases, which, during the breeding season, the bird broadcasts around the neighbourhood all day and sometimes for much of the night.

The male does most – although not all – of the singing. Studies have shown that unmated males are the most vocal, performing the greatest variety of songs and in the widest spread of directions in their hope of tempting a female away from her first choice. Females select males according to the quality of their song and their vigour in defending territory. However, this species has up to four broods per year, and partners may find new mates during the breeding season. Successful males expand their vocal repertoire as they grow older.

This species is one of 17 in the mockingbird family (Mimidae) and the only one widespread in the USA, its range extending to northeastern Canada and the Caribbean. Grey-brown in colour, and a little smaller than

a starling, it has a signature habit of raising its wings while hopping around in search of food. A bird of open country with scattered vegetation, it has adapted seamlessly to suburbia, where mown lawns offer perfect feeding grounds for snapping up small bugs, and shrubberies provide hidden nest sites in which to raise young – an average brood comprising four. Today, more than half the US population of mockingbirds breeds in urban areas.

Despite its widespread popularity, not everybody loves the northern mockingbird. This notoriously feisty species will readily attack hawks, cats and other animals, and may even train its sights on people if it perceives them as a threat to its nest. One incident in 2007 involving regular attacks on a postal carrier in Tulsa, Oklahoma, resulted in warning letters being sent around the neighbourhood. Research has found that mockingbirds recognize individuals who have approached their nest in the past, and will single them out for a special dive-bombing. Hardly the stuff of lullabies.

USA

Bald Eagle

Haliaeetus leucocephalus

'The founding fathers made an appropriate choice when they selected the bald eagle as the emblem of our nation,' wrote US President John F. Kennedy in 1961 to the National Audubon Society. 'The fierce beauty and proud independence of this great bird aptly symbolizes the strength and freedom of America,' he added, 'but as latter-day citizens we shall have failed a trust if we permit the eagle to disappear.'

This cultural clout has a long history. Native Americans had honoured the bald eagle since ancient times as a spiritual intermediary between humans and gods. The bird became officially iconic on 20 June 1782, when Congress – taking their lead from Imperial Rome – incorporated its image into the Great Seal of the United States, clutching an olive branch of peace in one foot and the arrows of war in the other. Today, as the emblem of the military, identified with such all-American values as power and freedom, its proud glare embodies the spirit of a nation.

Given this status, you might expect the bald eagle to have received special protection. By the mid-twentieth century, however, it was crashing towards extinction. Ironically, its bellicose reputation convinced farmers that it threatened their livestock, despite no evidence to support this. Open season was declared. In Alaska alone bounty hunters killed more than 100,000 bald eagles between 1917 and 1952. Pollution came next: in particular from DDT, a post-war agricultural insecticide, which raced through the food chain to cause egg-thinning and breeding failure. By the 1950s the bird's population had plummeted from an estimated 300,000–500,000 in the eighteenth century to only 412 pairs across the 48 contiguous states of the USA.

Happily, conservation prevailed. In 1967 the bald eagle was declared Endangered, and in 1972 DDT was banned. A dramatic recovery has since seen a 779 per cent increase over 40 years. In 1995 the eagle's conservation status was downgraded from Endangered to Threatened. In 2007 the bird was removed from both lists, and today it breeds in all contiguous US states, plus Alaska, Canada and Mexico's Baja California Peninsula.

The eagle behind the icon is not 'bald' at all. Its head is feathered in white, which, against its brown body and white tail, produces a piebald appearance that may explain the epithet. The ancient Greek scientific name *leucocephalus*, meaning 'white-headed', is more accurate. Either way, the bird is unmistakable. Measuring up to 2.4 metres (nearly 8 ft) across its broad wings, it is fractionally larger than the golden eagle (see page 83) and has a bright yellow bill. A fish-eater that uses fish-hook claws to pluck its catch from the surface, it also takes water birds, small mammals and carrion – especially in winter, when anything from dead livestock to beached whales makes the menu. It also pirates food from other predators, notably ospreys.

Bald eagles breed in wetlands, both coastal and inland, and choose a large mature tree in which to build the largest known stick nest of any bird. One record-breaker from Florida measured 2.9 metres (9½ ft) wide by 6 metres (nearly 20 ft) deep and weighed 1,814 kilograms (4,000 lb). Youngsters, typically two, remain around their parents for up to eight weeks after fledging. Once mature, they face few natural threats and may live 20 years or more – if people allow them.

Greater Sage Grouse

Centrocercus urophasianus

Just before dawn, an unearthly popping and bubbling wells up from the dark Wyoming prairie. The first rays reveal a cluster of chicken-like birds arranged around a clearing in the sagebrush. Flaunting extravagant fans and ruffles, they strut and bow in ritualized dance, each inflating and deflating two yellow, balloon-like air sacs on its chest to produce that weird sound. In the still air, the chorus carries for kilometres.

The birds are male greater sage grouse and the performance is their communal breeding display, called a lek. The smaller, dowdier females watch from the sidelines, running their eye over the talent on show. These leks take place during spring, and last for several hours every early morning and evening. Groups of 15–70 males gather on time-honoured display grounds, deep in the sagebrush. The competition is brutally hierarchical: one dominant male may mate with 80 per cent of the females, leaving many rivals unmated.

The bubbling of the sage-grouse lek was once as much a part of the American West as its thundering herds of bison. But the American West is not what it was. The sagebrush that once carpeted vast tracts of prairie has been steadily whittled away, millions of hectares lost to ranchland or, more recently, developments such as gas fields. This charismatic gamebird depends completely on the plant from which it gets its name, feeding on the soft leaves and buds, which in winter make up as much as 99 per cent of its diet, and using the dense thickets for its ground nests and roosting sites.

As sagebrush has disappeared, so has the greater sage grouse. It has lost 90 per cent of its range over the last century and, just like the bison, is now fighting to hold on to its ancestral home. Conservationists today estimate the population at about 150,000 birds, mostly confined to protected areas. The IUCN lists the species as Vulnerable. Many scientists believe it warrants upgrading to Endangered.

On the Wyoming prairie, the lekking season draws to a close and the males melt away into camouflaged anonymity. Now the females take over, tending their clutches of six to nine eggs and raising their broods. These youngsters leave the nest immediately they hatch. They start life feeding on insects but will soon graduate to sagebrush – if there is any left.

Purple Martin

Progne subis

Castles, apartment blocks, condominiums: few wild bird species have a more elaborate range of nesting options than the purple martin – and all laid on by human beings. For centuries, this synanthropic member of the swallow family has lived alongside people, taking advantage of the nesting spaces we have provided. Today, across most of the eastern and central United States and Canada, these purpose-built homes have become the *only* places in which the species breeds.

Housing purple martins is nothing new. Native American communities, including the Cherokees, Chickasaws and Choctaws, first fixed hollowed-out gourds on poles to provide such homes centuries ago. They had observed the benefits these aerial insect-eaters brought to the homestead, snapping up flies that swarmed over drying meat and mobbing any passing hawk that might be eyeing up the chickens. Their twittering song also provided a pleasant summer soundtrack.

Modern culture has run with this principle, using synthetic materials to manufacture everything from single gourd-shaped vessels to enormous boxes with individual compartments for dozens of pairs. In some towns, these huge structures, mounted on poles 3 metres (10 ft) above the ground to keep them out of the reach of cats and raccoons, are part of the architecture of suburbia. Each year the birds flock back to them, knowing they'll find a degree of safety by nesting close to humans.

Before *Homo sapiens* came along, purple martins used holes in tree stumps – a strategy that they still pursue in the southwestern USA. Today, in the east, however, most suitable natural holes are quickly taken by house sparrows (*Passer domesticus*) or European starlings (*Sturnus vulgaris*). These two rampant invasive species, both hole-nesters, always outcompete martins, if necessary destroying their eggs or young. Given that it was people who brought both to the Americas from Europe, it seems only right that we now provide alternative accommodation. Today householders can ensure that they attract the desired tenants by providing crescent-shaped entrances – disliked by starlings and sparrows – or by expelling the invaders.

The purple martin is a robust, short-tailed swallow, identified by the breeding male's iridescent blue-black (not purple) plumage. It breeds across eastern and central North America, northwards to southern Canada, with a few isolated populations in the west, and migrates south to overwinter in South America, largely in Brazil, making a journey of roughly 8,000 kilometres (5,000 miles) through either Central America or the Caribbean.

In spring, the first returning migrants reach their breeding colonies in Texas and Florida as early as late January. Males arrive first to claim territory and investigate nest sites, competing with others for the best chambers in a purpose-built block. Inside an apartment, a pair builds a nest of mud and twigs, lined with leaves. The female lays three to six eggs and both parents feed the nestlings, which fledge about a month after hatching. After breeding, purple martins gather in large flocks, typically on bridges or powerlines, feeding and roosting together as they prepare to head south. Their mass departures may be large enough to detect on radar.

Today, despite population crashes during the twentieth century – largely owing to those pesky sparrows and starlings – the IUCN lists the purple martin as Least Concern. However, conservationists worry that this species is now almost entirely dependent on nest boxes across the eastern half of North America, and that the practice of providing these artificial homes is becoming less popular with younger generations.

Wild Turkey

Meleagris gallopavo

Y ou might be forgiven for supposing that the huge domestic fowl at the heart of a British Christmas dinner is of eastern origin, given its name. This supposition is echoed in other languages, with the bird's name in French (*dinde*: 'from India') and Russian (*indyushka*: 'bird of India') suggesting an even more easterly provenance.

In fact, this hefty gamebird, now bred for our consumption worldwide, is American. Indeed, it is *so* American that Benjamin Franklin once mused that it would make a better national emblem – 'a bird of courage, though a little vain and silly' – than the bald eagle (see page 98), which he judged as being of 'bad moral character'. Long before Franklin, the wild turkey had been part of Native American culture; it was domesticated by the Aztecs by at least 800 BC, and subsequently by indigenous peoples further north.

As for the name, it was early Spanish settlers who first returned with the bird to the Old World, but Turkish traders from the Levant who were responsible for introducing it more widely around Europe. From Shakespeare, it is clear that the bird was known in England by 1602. 'Contemplation makes a rare turkey-cock of him,' says Fabian of Malvolio in *Twelfth Night*: 'how he jets under his advanced plumes!'

This species is one of two turkeys that make up the genus *Meleagris* – the other being the ocellated turkey (*M. ocellata*) of Central America, which has never been domesticated – and is the heaviest member of the Galliformes, the order that comprises pheasants and other gamebirds. Although wild birds are smaller than their domesticated relatives, they are still pretty big, with males weighing up to 11 kilograms (24 lb). As with all gamebirds, cocks are larger and more colourful than hens. They appear at their finest during the breeding season, with their glossy, iridescent upperparts and the strange protuberances from their naked red head. The latter include a throat wattle and an extensible flap over the bill, called a snood, that enlarges when the bird becomes excited. The long tail feathers spread into an impressive fan, and were prized by indigenous communities for their ornamental value.

Wild turkeys are woodland birds, preferring areas with clearings, where they forage for acorns, seeds and small animals. They once roamed in countless millions across the continent, from central Mexico to southeastern Canada, but deforestation and heavy hunting caused their numbers to plummet to 30,000 by the 1930s. Conservation has since helped to raise the population to an estimated 7 million. In some areas they are now very tame, approaching people for handouts and even becoming aggressive during the breeding season, when the gobbling of displaying males can be heard from up to 1 kilometre (½ mile) away. Although ground-nesters, like all gamebirds, they are perfectly capable of flight, roosting every night in tall trees to avoid the likes of prowling bobcats.

Today it is America, unsurprisingly, that eats the most turkey. An estimated 46 million of the domesticated birds are consumed every Thanksgiving and another 20 million or so every Christmas and Easter. Worldwide, the consumption of turkey meat – now processed in many different forms – has doubled since the 1970s. The same cannot be said of Brussels sprouts.

Common Loon

Gavia immer

You'll have heard the call of the common loon whether you know it or not. A high, quivering tremolo, haunting and other-worldly, it has become a movie soundtrack signifier: to solitude and wilderness what the hoot of a tawny owl is to darkness and suspense. In *On Golden Pond* Katharine Hepburn tried, rather ineptly, to imitate one. But at least, beside a New England lake, she was in the right place. In *Raiders of the Lost Ark* and *Out of Africa* the directors had no such excuse.

This big water bird is the living embodiment of North America's northern lakes, its haunting calls and exquisite breeding plumage the subject of ancient folklore and iconography. For the Ojibwe people, the loon was the creator of the world. The myth of its necklace – the spangle of black-and-white markings around its throat – is shared by many First Nations peoples, and tells how the bird was given this adornment in return for restoring to a Tsimshian medicine man the gift of sight. Today the common loon is celebrated as the provincial bird of Ontario, the province that is home to more than half the breeding population, and appears on the Canadian one-dollar coin, known as a 'loonie'.

The origins of the name 'loon' are uncertain. It might derive from the Old Norse *lómr* or it might simply be a comic description of the bird's awkward movements on land, with feet placed so far back that it cannot walk properly. Either way, loons are known in Europe as divers – a name that describes their hunting behaviour, in which they submerge to depths of 60 metres (nearly 200 ft) and pursue fish with great speed and agility. In Europe, the common loon is known as the great northern diver. It is the largest of five species worldwide and cuts a distinctive profile as it swims low in the water, with prominent head and dagger bill. In breeding plumage, its blue-black upperparts are beautifully marked with white checks and spots – a mantle that it sheds in winter.

Common loons breed across much of the northern USA and Canada, their range extending from 48°N to the Arctic Circle, with smaller populations in southern Greenland, Iceland and Svalbard. Prime breeding habitat comprises forested freshwater lakes, replete with fish and affording enough room for a take-off runway along the surface – a necessity for this heavy bird. Pairs are extremely territorial, and will claim a whole lake or bay for themselves. A variety of far-carrying calls, including wailing, yodelling and those Hepburn tremolos, continue day and night and serve to assert ownership and keep in contact. The female lays two eggs, on average, and incubation lasts 28 days. The chicks can dive within days of hatching, but can't fly for seven or eight weeks, and when still small may ride on their parents' backs. The adults are fiercely protective at this time and will use their bills to defend their brood against predators as large as foxes. In July 2019, a dead bald eagle retrieved in Bridgton, Maine, was found to bear fatal stab wounds from the bill of a common loon.

Soon after breeding, common loons head south to coasts, bays and unfrozen inland water bodies. Birds from western Canada head down the Pacific coast as far as Baja California, those from central regions reach the Gulf of Mexico, and those from the east head down the Atlantic seaboard or cross to northwestern Europe. In their winter quarters pairs separate and fall silent. In spring, however, they reunite on their northern breeding lakes and the wilderness soundtrack resumes.

Snow Goose

Anser caerulescens

O n a chilly April dawn in Manitoba, southern Canada, an impatient murmuring drifts across the fields. The sky lightens and the sound swells, building to a jet-engine roar. Then, as the sun emerges, it explodes into a cackling cacophony. Thousands of birds are taking flight, launching skywards from the dark horizon. At first, they almost blot out the sky, milling overhead in a blizzard of wings. Then the mass separates into straggling lines, each heading towards the feeding grounds.

Snow geese spend more than half of their lives on the move, migrating north every spring to breeding grounds in the high Arctic, then returning in autumn to overwinter on farmland and coastal plains as far south as Texas. En route, they use traditional wetland pit stops. Tens of thousands assemble, creating one of North America's most impressive wildlife spectacles as they commute daily between roosting and feeding grounds.

This medium-sized goose gets its name from its snow-white plumage, relieved only by black wingtips, pink bill and rose-red feet and legs. It also occurs in a smoky blue-grey colour morph, known as the blue goose. Irrespective of colour, scientists recognize two races. The lesser snow goose (*A. c. caerulescens*) is slightly smaller and much more numerous. It breeds from central northern Canada west across the Bering Strait to northeastern Siberia, and its winter quarters span the southern USA, from California to the Gulf Coast of Texas (although the Siberian birds winter in British Columbia). The greater snow goose (*A. c. atlanticus*) breeds in northeastern Canada and Greenland, and winters on the Atlantic coastal plain, southwards to North Carolina.

Migrating snow geese travel in family groups that coalesce into larger flocks at pit stops. They may cover over 1,000 kilometres (620 miles) a day, keeping in contact using honking calls. Once on their tundra breeding grounds, each pair claims its own territory within a large colony that may contain several thousand pairs. Nesting starts from late May, once the ice has thawed. The female lays her eggs in a shallow depression lined with plant material and down, and the youngsters hatch after 22–25 days, leaving the nest a few days later. Parents defend chicks against nest-raiders such as Arctic foxes, and snow geese sometimes nest close to snowy owls (*Bubo scandiacus*) in order to gain protection from the proximity of this formidable predator.

Snow geese are voracious, spending over 50 per cent of their time feeding. In the Arctic, they subsist largely on grasses. In winter, however, many have shifted their coastal feeding grounds inland to feed on leftover grain, causing numbers to soar; today's population of some 6 million lesser snow geese is three times that of the 1970s and is having a serious impact on the bird's tundra breeding habitat, especially around Hudson Bay. In 1999 Canada relaxed hunting restrictions with the aim of reducing populations to sustainable levels. So far, however, the numbers continue to rise, and the annual white blizzard shows no sign of abating.

Great Grey Owl

Strix nebulosa

Wise owls – if you believe the old adage – surely don't come wiser than this one. Yes, all owls appear to have expressions, courtesy of their big forward-facing eyes and facial markings. But whereas some species project ferocity or anger, the great grey exudes intellectual curiosity. You almost expect it to peer over a pair of bifocals.

This wisdom exists only in our imagination, of course: an impression triggered by the white eyebrows and concentric rings that surround the bird's penetrating yellow eyes, and accentuated by its black goatee beard and huge brainbox head – the largest of any owl. In reality, the great grey owl's facial disc is a satellite dish-like adaptation to boost its phenomenal hearing; this bird can locate and capture by sound alone a vole creeping along 60 centimetres (24 in) beneath the surface of the snow. That soft cloak of smoky grey-brown plumage exaggerates the head's real size. Indeed, in its entirety this owl – at up to 80 centimetres (32 in) the longest on average of all the world's owls – is not quite as big as it appears. Most eagle owls (genus *Bubo*) have shorter tails, but are heavier and more powerful.

Wise or not, this elusive bird of twilight and shadows embodies Canada's northern forests. It looms large in First Nations folklore and goes by a variety of folk names, including 'spectral owl' and 'phantom of the north'. Fittingly, it was in Canada that this species was first described to science in the late eighteenth century, and today it is the provincial bird of Manitoba. However, the bird's range extends far beyond Canada, south through the forested mountains of the western United States and – in a separate race – east across the forests of Eurasia, from Scandinavia to Siberia.

Great grey owls frequent various types of forest, notably spruce and birch, but always require clearings in which to hunt, with stumps for perches and gnarled old trees for nesting and roosting. Their staple diet is small rodents, typically lemmings and voles, which they hunt either from a perch or by flying low over clearings, scrutinizing the ground below. This species has perfected the 'snow plunge', diving feet-first through snow to grab a hidden victim it has detected underneath. When the rodent supply runs out – a periodic upshot of the animals' boom–bust breeding cycle – the owls head south. 'Irruption' years sometimes occur: in the winter of 2004–5 some 5,000 great grey owls were recorded in Minnesota, 13 times the previous state record.

Courtship gets under way in spring with the male's deep, rhythmic hooting. A pair generally take over the old stick nest of another bird, but may also use a hollow in the top of a tall tree stump. Conservationists have found that artificial nests will also do – even a dog basket placed high in the branches. The female lays four eggs, on average, although she may not lay at all during poor rodent years. Incubation lasts some 30 days, and the female guards her young for another two or three weeks while the male provisions them with food. After fledging, the youngsters hang around the nest site for at least another two months, their parents protecting them aggressively from predators.

Internationally, the great grey owl is listed as Least Concern. However, its numbers fluctuate significantly with vole populations, and the species is under threat from modern timber management, in which suitable nesting trees and deadwood perches are removed and forest gaps planted over. Canada remains a stronghold, home to more than half the estimated worldwide population of 60,000 individuals. It may yet require a little more wisdom from foresters to keep things that way.

Greater Roadrunner

Geococcyx californianus

For several generations of children – and, doubtless, plenty of parents – it was a Warner Brothers cartoon that put this bird on the map. *Wile E. Coyote and the Road Runner*, originally created by animation director Chuck Jones and writer Michael Maltese, ran from 1948 to 2014, and featured the ever more elaborate but always doomed attempts of the hapless canine to capture his fleet-footed avian quarry.

In real life, the greater roadrunner does not say 'beep beep!' Neither does it bear the scientific name *Boulevardus burnupius*. Otherwise, however, the cartoon was not so wide of the mark. This ground-dwelling relative of the cuckoos is indeed the Usain Bolt of flying birds, sometimes topping 30 kph (18 mph) as it dashes across the ground. Flying is a last resort, and those short wings are good for only a few airborne seconds at a time.

The greater roadrunner is native to the chapparal, the semi-desert scrublands that carpet much of Mexico and the southern USA. In Mexico, tradition holds that the bird was a bringer of babies, like the white stork (see page 56) in Europe, and indigenous Pueblo communities saw the bird as a protector against evil spirits. To ornithologists, this is the larger of two similar species that both belong to the cuckoo family (Cuculidae). It looks little like your average cuckoo, with its long legs and terrestrial habits – although, like all cuckoos, it has zygodactyl toes: that is to say, two facing forward and two back. It is some 50–60 centimetres (20–24 in) in length, its most striking features a jaunty, cocked tail and crest.

Roadrunners capture prey in lightning dashes, running with head and tail stretched out parallel to the ground. Victims range from insects and scorpions to reptiles and small mammals. The bird will even tackle small rattlesnakes, seizing the serpent by the tail and whip-cracking its head against the ground, and has reflexes fast enough to pluck a dragonfly from the air. Food goes down whole, with a length of snake sometimes left dangling from the bill as the rest is digested inside.

These birds are well adapted to their arid environment, able to reabsorb water from their faeces before excreting it, and to use special glands in front of their eyes to eliminate salt from their water intake. Deserts can also be freezing, so roadrunners sunbathe in the morning after a cold night, fluffing out their back feathers to expose the black skin underneath and absorb more solar energy.

In spring, a male courts his partner with cooing song, wagging wings and dangled food gifts. Unlike some cuckoos, roadrunners are not brood parasites but generally build their own nest in a bush or cactus. The male gathers materials while his mate focuses on construction and lays two to eight pale eggs. The youngsters fledge some 18 days after hatching but will hang around for another fortnight, cadging food.

Speed also helps roadrunners to escape danger – not just Wile E. Coyote, but a range of predators that include skunks, house cats and raptors. A clattering of the bill sounds the alarm. Ironically, the greatest threat to this species may come from roads – not just traffic, but also the proliferation of new highways, which fragments populations. Hard winters can also prove disastrous: roadrunners do not migrate, so a serious ice-over can prove deadlier than any pesky coyote.

Crested Caracara

Caracara plancus

Official sources state that the national bird of Mexico is the golden eagle (see page 83). The proof is there on the national flag, where this big raptor perches with wings spread against the heraldic bands of white, red and green. But is the bird depicted really an eagle? The celebrated Mexican ornithologist Rafael Martín del Campo (1910–1987) proposed that it should actually be seen as a crested caracara – a smaller raptor, but one that enjoys a closer association with the country. The bird was known to be sacred to the Aztecs, after all, and was depicted on pre-Columbian codices. Its feathers were once used for the ceremonial headdresses of priests, and its beak and claws ground into powder for an aphrodisiac.

Whatever its official status, the caracara is a much more familiar bird to most Mexicans than is the eagle. This is a medium-sized raptor, with long legs, black-and-white plumage and a naked face that flushes red or yellow according to age – or mood. It inhabits open country, from semi-desert to ranchland and coastal plains, and is often seen hopping across the ground or perched conspicuously atop a cactus, betraying its presence with the rattling call from which it gets its name. Beyond Mexico, its range extends from the southern tip of South America through Central America to the southern USA, where it is common in southern Texas.

The crested caracara is primarily a scavenger, its naked face an adaptation – like that of the vultures alongside which it often feeds – to prevent the fouling of its feathers when poking around inside a bloody carcass. This bird is not a vulture, however, but belongs with the falcons in the family Falconidae. Unlike typical falcons, it does not zoom after prey in flight but instead uses its shorter, broader wings to carry it on low foraging sorties, often arriving at carcasses before vultures, then bullying away the larger competition. Long legs allow it to forage on the ground, where everything from jackrabbits to tarantulas is fair game. Working together, groups may overpower prey as large as a skunk or boa constrictor, striking lethal blows with their powerful feet.

Breeding starts noisily, as a pair throw back their heads in tandem to utter their guttural courtship calls. Their nest is either reappropriated from another bird or assembled untidily from sticks and grasses, typically in desert plants such as mesquites and cacti, and often festooned with animal remains. The female lays two or three eggs, which she incubates for 28–32 days, during which time both birds defend the nest against raiders such as raccoons. Youngsters remain with their parents for a few weeks after fledging, and family parties may band together into larger groups that roost and forage communally.

In 1999, taxonomists briefly split this species into two: the northern crested caracara (*C. cheriway*) and the southern crested caracara (*C. plancus*). They have since reclassified these as simply geographical races of the same species. Today both are faring reasonably well, listed by the IUCN as Least Concern. But should conservationists become complacent, they need only remember the fate of the now-extinct Guadalupe caracara (*C. lutosa*), which enjoys the dubious distinction of being the only known bird to have been intentionally exterminated by humans. It was dubbed 'evil' and 'vicious' by settlers on Mexico's Guadalupe Island for its attacks on their introduced goats, and the last one was seen alive in 1903.

Green Jay

Cyanocorax yncas

A machine-gun rattle of harsh, metallic calls resounds from a mesquite bush – *churr, churr, churr* – prompting a response from the next thicket. A bird drops to the dusty ground in a flurry of green and blue. It hops about briefly, poking impatiently at a fallen seed pod, before bounding to the next bush with a flash of its vivid yellow tail. Two birds follow in floppy-winged flight and are quickly swallowed by the foliage. Then two more, calling insistently as they catch up with the gang.

A feeding party of green jays demands attention. These lively birds are constantly on the move as they work their scrubby habitat, seeking out anything edible – fruits, seeds, insects – while communicating in a variety of calls, both melodic and dissonant. In plain view, their rich greens and yellows are set off by a dashing black face mask and a splash of electric blue on crown and cheeks. When lying low, however, they can disappear, that plumage patchwork offering subtle camouflage among the greenery.

Jays belong to the corvid family and, like crows and magpies, are highly intelligent. This species is no exception. Watch a feeding party and their curiosity is soon evident. Study them for longer, as scientists have done, and you will discover just how far their talents extend. This species is one of the few North American birds known to use tools, deploying small twigs to prise up bark and winkle out food. Like other jays, it also caches food for later retrieval, while its extensive vocal repertoire even extends to mimicking hawks, in order both to scare away rivals and to panic other birds into abandoning their own finds.

Green jays frequent scrubby bush, parks and open woodland. Come April, a pair build their stick nest deep in a thorny thicket. The brood of three to five chicks receive a helping hand from their yearling siblings – the previous year's brood, which have stuck around to help their parents defend the territory. Once the new brood have fledged, the parents drive away these adolescent hangers-on to start a new life of their own.

This species ranges from Bolivia to southern Texas, where it brings a splash of Latin flair to the Lone Star state. However, it is in Mexico that it is best known – notably, in the Yucatán Peninsula, where it has inspired the Green Jay Mayan Birding Club. Today this community initiative – championed by its eye-catching ambassador – has grown from humble roots to exert significant influence on conservation across the peninsula.

Hoatzin

Opisthocomus hoazin

An animal's nicknames generally suggest how much of an impression it makes, and this bizarre species has acquired plenty. 'Reptile bird', 'skunk bird' and 'stink bird' are among them, as is 'Canje pheasant' – Canje being a region of Guyana, where this is the national bird.

The hoatzin is not a pheasant, although its superficial likeness, with long tail, stubby wings and small head, once meant it was classified among the Galliformes (gamebirds). Nailing its true identity has proved tricky. Subsequent theories allied the species with cuckoos, turacos and even doves. Neither DNA evidence nor the fossil record has since provided any conclusive answer, and today many taxonomists are happy to treat this oddity as the sole member of its own order, the Opisthocomiformes.

Whatever the taxonomic truth, the hoatzin is an intriguing creature. At first glance, 'reptile bird' seems apt. Indeed, with its short wings, long tail, spiky crest and naked blue face, it bears an uncanny resemblance to artists' impressions of *Archaeopteryx*, the prehistoric ancestor of all feathered things. This likeness prompted early scientists to speculate that the hoatzin represents a missing link between reptiles and birds – speculation intensified by the discovery that chicks hatch with two claws on each wing, one each on the first and second digits.

In fact, these claws are a relatively recent adaptation, rather than some evolutionary relic. Hoatzins inhabit tropical swamp forests, typically in quiet backwaters, where they construct their flimsy stick nests overhanging the water. When danger appears, such as snakes or raptors, the adults flap noisily away and abandon the chicks to their fate. The chicks, however, have an exit strategy: they drop into the water below, drift a little way downstream, then use their claws – along with their bill and feet – to haul themselves back out, returning to the nest once the danger has passed.

The name 'stink bird' comes down to food-processing. The hoatzin feeds largely on the leaves of marsh plants, such as arums, using a unique digestive system called 'foregut fermentation' to handle this cellulose heavy diet. Simply put, the food ferments and breaks down in the bird's modified crop en route to its stomach. This technique has its drawbacks. First, the hoatzin has had to scale down the key flight apparatus of pectoral muscles and sternum in order to accommodate the enlarged crop, so is a poor flyer. Second, fermentation stinks: the bird smells like manure.

When feeding, hoatzins clamber clumsily through the foliage, their presence often betrayed by their wheezy call. A feathered lump at the base of their crop helps them balance on branches, a technique called sternal perching. A pair raises an average brood of two. The wing claws disappear long before the chicks reach adulthood, and for two years these youngsters act as assistants to their parents, babysitting the next brood and helping to feed them a smelly soup of regurgitated, fermented leaves.

Outside Guyana, hoatzins range widely across northern South America, notably in the Amazon and Orinoco basins. Populations are largely stable, although habitat loss is always a threat. Some indigenous peoples have traditionally harvested the bird's feathers and eggs, but its reputedly foul taste has kept it off most menus.

Hyacinth Macaw

Anodorhynchus hyacinthinus

Araucous screeching heralds the arrival of the 'King of Parrots'. On cue, two big, blue birds flap steadily into view and alight in a tall manduvi tree, fanning their long tails wide. Up in the branches the conversation continues, male and female muttering as they settle down. Soon they are preening each other with their massive, nutcracker bills.

In the heart of Brazil's Pantanal – the vast wetland in the country's southwest – you can hardly miss the hyacinth macaw. Noisy and conspicuous, it might appear to be thriving. Sadly, it isn't. With a world population estimated at no more than 6,500 individuals, this magnificent bird is a victim of both habitat loss and poaching for the illegal cage-bird trade, in which adults can fetch more than US$1,000. An estimated 10,000 were taken from the wild in the 1980s, and today the IUCN lists the species as Vulnerable – one of 46 of the world's 145 parrot species threatened with extinction.

The Pantanal is the largest of three regions in Brazil where this species still occurs. Here it subsists largely on palm nuts, notably those of *Acrocomia aculeata* and *Attalea phalerata*, using its powerful bill to break into fruit that would defy a hammer, and its muscular tongue to prise out the contents. Pairs mate for life, nesting in tree holes and generally producing a single chick each season. This youngster fledges after around 110 days and remains with its parents for six months, not breeding until its seventh year.

At nearly 1 metre (3 ft) in length, this is the longest of the world's parrots and pipped as the heaviest only by New Zealand's flightless kakapo (see page 192). Unmistakable, with its dazzling blue livery set off by canary-yellow flashes of naked skin around eye and bill, it is a long-lived, highly intelligent bird with no natural predators. At the heart of its ecology is a strange dichotomy, however: the macaw depends on the toco toucan (*Ramphastos toco*) to disperse the seeds of the manduvi trees in which it nests, yet this same toucan is the principal predator of the macaw's eggs.

Today conservationists are working to protect the hyacinth macaw across its range, both through shoring up nesting habitat and by tackling poaching and trafficking. On the macaw's side is its popularity. This spectacular bird is welcomed on to local ranches, where pairs may take up residence for years, sometimes using nest boxes. With ecotourism now rivalling cattle-ranching in the Pantanal's economy, looking after these crowd-pleasing parrots is beginning to pay its way.

Andean Cock-of-the-rock

Rupicola peruvianus

T he voices are nothing special: a wheezy belching that drifts up from the pre-dawn murk like a chorus of asthmatic frogs. The singers, however, are something else. At first, they are visible only by colour, disembodied fireballs bobbing like lanterns in the forest gloom. But first light soon brings definition, revealing a dozen or so dove-sized birds, decked out in fluorescent scarlet and hopping from branch to branch in practised routine. Your binoculars pick out mad white eyes and bizarre feathered face-fans as each takes its turn centre stage.

These outlandish creatures are Andean cock-of-the-rocks. Their routine is the lek, a form of communal courtship display practised by a select group of animals around the world, in which males strut their stuff around a time-honoured arena before an audience of watching females, who take their pick from the talent on display. Here in the misty Peruvian cloud forest it happens on the same stage every breeding season, and has done for generations. The males gather for their lek in the half-light of early morning, and return at dusk for a repeat performance when the light reaches that exact intensity once more.

The Andean cock-of-the-rock was officially proclaimed the national bird of Peru in 1941. However, this remarkable species – known as *tunki* to the indigenous Quechua peoples – had been held in high esteem for centuries. The bird's finery is thought to have inspired the Incas' ceremonial scarlet robes and elaborate crested helmets, and perhaps even their practice of manipulating children's skulls into a more elongated shape by binding them with stones during early infancy.

To ornithologists, this is one of two similar species, the other being the Guianan cock-of-the-rock (*R. rupicola*) of the Amazon lowlands, both of which belong to the Cotingidae family of Latin-American songbirds. It inhabits higher elevations than its sister species, being found 500–2,400 metres (1,640–7,900 ft) up in the steep, moss-festooned forests of the eastern Andes, from Venezuela to Bolivia. Both, however, perform in leks. Males are polygamous and put all their efforts into these displays. Once suitors are chosen and mating accomplished, females are left to complete the breeding process alone. They build a cup nest of mud and saliva in the entrance to a cave or crevice (hence 'of the rock'), and produce a clutch of two white eggs, which they incubate for 25–28 days.

Away from the courtship arena, this is a shy bird that is surprisingly inconspicuous as it forages for fruit and insects in the mid-storey of the cloud forest, occasionally taking small frogs and other vertebrate prey. Research has shown that its droppings play an important role in seed dispersal, and its lek sites are often planted with flora that it has – in effect – cultivated there.

Back at the morning's show, the drama is over after an hour or so, the performers melting away backstage before the house lights turn their dazzling outfits into targets for boa constrictors or ocelots. Today, graver threats than these predators come in the form of habitat loss. But with a healthy population, the bird enjoys a conservation status of Least Concern, secure for now as a suitably splendid national icon.

Resplendent Quetzal

Pharomachrus mocinno

The indigenous peoples of Meso-America venerated this bird as the 'snake god' Quetzalcoatl. To the Aztecs and Mayans, it symbolized freedom and light, and the male's long emerald plumes, replicated in their headdresses, were thought to herald new growth in spring. The folk hero Tecún Umán, one of the last rulers of the K'iche' Maya in the highlands of what is now Guatemala, was said to have had his quetzal spirit guide hovering above him as he fought the Spanish; when he was eventually killed, the bird dipped its feathers in his blood, hence its scarlet breast. Before the conquistadors, legend has it, the bird was a beautiful singer. It has been silent ever since their arrival, and will not sing again until the land is freed.

Myth aside, the resplendent quetzal is the largest member of the trogon family (Trogonidae), which occurs in tropical forests worldwide. It was first described to science in 1832 by the Mexican naturalist Pablo de la Llave, who took the name from *quetzalli* – which, in the Nahuatl language of the Aztecs, meant 'upstanding plume'. Science, however, can't do justice to the sheer splendour of the pigeon-sized male. His iridescent green upperparts shimmer gold or violet with the light and are set off by scarlet underparts, a bright yellow bill, a helmet-like crest and, most impressive, fabulous 65-centimetre-long (26 in) emerald outer-tail coverts, which snake behind him as he flutters between branches in his misty, mossy cloud-forest home.

This is a bird of high altitudes, its relatively small population scattered through the mountains along the Cordillera Centroamericana, from southern Mexico to western Panama. Primarily a fruit eater, like all trogons, it feeds largely on wild avocados and other members of the Lauraceae family, swallowing the fruit whole and regurgitating the pips. And while it may not be a beautiful singer, it often reveals its presence in the canopy with a repeated three-syllable call, rather like the whimpering of a puppy.

Quetzal pairs are monogamous and territorial, excavating their nest in the rotten wood of an old tree stump. Breeding takes place from March to June. The male and female take turns to incubate the two eggs, the male's long plumes folding back over his head and out of the hole to resemble a tree fern, but the female – a duller green, without the plumes – departs before the chicks have fledged, leaving her mate to finish the process. Young males must wait three years to acquire their full finery.

Today the resplendent quetzal is the national bird of Guatemala and enshrined in the country's currency. It is uncommon and elusive, however, and listed by the IUCN as Near Threatened. Birdwatchers in search of a sighting might also try Costa Rica, where Monteverde Cloud Forest Biological Preserve is perhaps the best-known hotspot. Habitat loss remains a threat everywhere, since the quetzal requires undisturbed tracts of forest with enough crumbling tree stumps for nest sites. Even in prime terrain, it can be hard to find – when it is perched quietly, those iridescent greens mimic the gleaming foliage of the wet forest canopy – but once spotted, it is seldom forgotten.

Andean Condor

Vultur gryphus

F ew animals and landscapes are more inseparable in our imaginations than this immense bird and the Andes mountains in which it lives. For any watcher of wildlife documentaries, the very word 'condor' conjures an instant soundtrack of panpipes. Bird and location seem yoked together in a celebration of wilderness and scale.

The Andean condor is the world's largest flying bird, if size is judged by wingspan and weight combined. Its wings may measure 3.3 metres (nearly 11 ft) from tip to tip – only certain albatrosses can exceed this – while a male's average weight of 12.5 kilograms (27½ lb) is topped only by the males of two or three bustard (Otididae) species. The condor's great wing area, the largest of any bird, enables it to capture the thermals and updraughts of its mountain home and soar for many miles over the peaks and canyons with barely a flap.

Size apart, this huge bird is unmistakable. The jet-black plumage of adults is relieved by a thick Shakespearean ruff of white feathers around the neck and broad white panels on the wings. The naked head – an adaptation to prevent the soiling of any plumage when probing a carcass – carries an inflatable throat wattle and a comb on top, and the greyish face blushes a brighter red when the bird becomes excited, such as during its hopping, clucking courtship displays.

The Andean condor is the largest of the New World vultures (Cathartidae). Whether these birds are related to the Old World vultures of Africa and Eurasia, or have simply acquired similar traits through convergent evolution, remains a hot debate among taxonomists. Either way, the two groups resemble each other in both appearance and lifestyle. Andean condors feed almost entirely on large carcasses, once mostly those of large wild mammals, such as guanacos and deer, but today increasingly on dead livestock. Their acute sense of smell – unusual in birds – enables them to detect decomposing flesh from afar. Individuals may cover 200 kilometres (125 miles) a day in their search for food, and may be led to carrion by smaller species, such as turkey vultures (*Cathartes aura*), which in turn rely on the condor's greater power and bigger bill to open up a large carcass. A condor may go for days without eating, but equally may eat so much at one sitting that it can barely get airborne. Birds may gather at big carcasses, notably those of beached whales along the coast of Chile.

This is a mountain species, although it may visit lowlands to scavenge. Pairs, which mate for life, nest on rock ledges in the 3,000–5,000 metre (9,800–16,400 ft) altitude zone. They produce one or two chicks a year, which can fly at six months. With no natural predators and a slow reproductive rate, this is one of the world's longest-lived birds: Theo, a captive condor that died in Connecticut Zoo in 2010 aged 79, is the oldest bird ever known.

Andean condors range from Venezuela southwards to Tierra del Fuego, at the continent's southern tip. The bird has loomed large in the culture of this whole region since at least 2500 BC. Mythologized in ancient times as a sun deity, it once played a key role in ceremony and today appears on the coats of arms of seven nations, including Chile. Sadly, the bird's iconic status has not halted its decline. Today it is extremely rare in the north, and the majority of the 6,700 or so remaining individuals are in Chile and Argentina. Even there, it remains vulnerable, both to habitat loss and secondary poisoning; in one incident in 2018, some 34 condors died alongside a puma at a poisoned carcass set to kill the cat. With the bird now listed as Vulnerable, conservation efforts are under way, including captive incubation and wild reintroduction schemes. Scientists hope for success – otherwise, with no condors over the Andes, that panpipe celebration might just sound more like a lament.

Torrent Duck

Merganetta armata

In the wild white waters of the high Andes, the torrent duck has taken on the role of stunt kayaker, flinging itself headlong into the maelstrom with apparent abandon. This can be alarming to witness. But, just as the birds appear to have drowned or been dashed to pieces, they bob back to the surface, miraculously unharmed.

This bird belongs to the shelduck subfamily of ducks (Tadorninae) and is endemic to the Andes, inhabiting fast-flowing mountain streams along the length of the range. Although further south it may appear at sea-level, in Bolivia and other central regions it is a bird of high altitude, choosing habitats that to most other species would, frankly, be hazardous.

The incentive for this lifestyle of derring-do is, of course, food. The torrent duck feeds on aquatic invertebrates such as stonefly larvae that are themselves specially adapted to the turbulent conditions. With no natural competitors able to brave the torrent, the birds have this diet to themselves, plunging beneath the surface to probe under rocks and even feeding directly under the cascade of a waterfall.

Even without this remarkable behaviour, torrent ducks would be distinctive. Males sport a boldly striped head and neck and a bright-red bill. Females have a yellow bill and underparts of rich rusty orange. Both sexes have a long and unusually stiff tail, which serves both as a powerful rudder in the turbulent waters and as a brace against the slippery surface of the rocks on which the birds perch.

Torrent ducks form long-term pair bonds, communicating through a shrill whistle (in the male) or a throaty squawk (the female). During courtship, males compete for partners with a leaping, splashing display along the water's surface. Once established, pairs nest close to the water, usually in a hidden crevice among the overhanging rocks, which they line with dry grass and down. The clutch of three or four eggs takes 43–44 days to incubate – one of the longest periods of any duck – and the male takes an active role in the incubation and rearing of the chicks.

As soon as these youngsters hatch, their life of adventure sports begins – typically starting with a headlong leap into the torrent below the nest. True to type, they invariably pop up again unharmed – although the parents have their work cut out in the early days to ensure that these stripy bundles of fluff are not whisked away downstream and out of sight.

Sword-billed Hummingbird

Ensifera ensifera

E cuador is blessed with some 135 species of hummingbird, accounting for 8.5 per cent of the nation's impressive roll call of bird species. The variety is dazzling, literally, and includes such feathered gems as the spangled coquette, empress brilliant and rainbow starfrontlet. By comparison with such beauties, the sword-billed hummingbird's green and brown plumage is rather drab. But what it lacks in coloration, it more than makes up for in its bill.

This species has, proportionally, the longest bill of any bird in the world. More medieval jousting lance than sword, it is – at up to 12 centimetres (4¾ in) – the only bill that accounts for more than half the total length of its owner. At rest, the poor bird must perch with its bill held up at an almost vertical angle to prevent itself from overbalancing. When preening, it must resort to using its feet.

Of course, this extraordinary appendage did not evolve merely to inconvenience its owner, but is a specialized tool for probing flowers for nectar. Every hummingbird species has a bill adapted to exploit particular blooms: some short and sharp; some long and curved. The exceptional length of the sword-billed hummingbird's enables it to probe deep into flowers with the longest corollas, notably *Passiflora mixta*, the nectar of which is inaccessible to all other species.

Like all hummingbirds, this species feeds while hovering in mid-air in front of its food plants, and visiting the same flowers in a continually repeated sequence, thus helping to ensure cross-pollination of the plant. Whirring wings hold it stationary while the bill reaches up into the hanging petals, the protrusible, grooved tongue flickering in and out beyond the tip to lap up nectar that no other hummer can reach.

Hummingbirds of all species live a high-octane life, and this one is no exception. Their metabolism runs faster than that of all other vertebrates in order to generate the energy necessary to beat their wings, and the heart rate of some species has been measured at more than 1,200 beats per minute. Just to survive, they must consume more than their own weight in nectar daily. This entails visiting hundreds of flowers. At any moment they are just hours from starvation, and they can only just store enough energy to survive overnight (when they enter a torpid state in which their heart rate and breathing slow dramatically).

As with all hummingbirds, the female of this species – distinguished from the male by her white belly – shoulders most of the burden of breeding. It is she who builds the neat, cup-shaped nest from moss and foliage, using spider silk to bind it together (which also allows it to expand as the young grow) and secure it to the branch. When her two eggs hatch, she feeds her nestlings on small arthropods and nectar by regurgitating the food into their open gapes.

The sword-billed hummingbird inhabits the temperate zone of montane cloud forest at altitudes of 1,700–3,500 metres (5,500–11,500 ft). Outside Ecuador, it occurs south to Bolivia and north to Venezuela. It is most easily found in forest edges and clearings – anywhere that its nectar plants grow in abundance. At present the population appears to be stable – the species is listed as Least Concern by the IUCN – but deforestation and climate change remain potential threats.

Tororoi Bailador

Grallaricula sp.

It might seem perverse to choose this obscure species to represent Colombia. This is the nation with a greater variety of birds than any other, after all, its total of 1,958 species (at the last count) representing nearly one fifth of the planet's total. Given the pageant of toucans, trogons and other splendours on offer, why would you single out this drab little oddity? At the time of writing, it doesn't even have a formal scientific name.

Tororoi bailador translates to 'dancing antpitta'. And this lack of an scientific name points to what makes the bird so special: the species was only identified in 2019, so there simply hasn't yet been time to give it one. Discovered in 2017 in Los Farallones de Cali National Park in Colombia's southwest, this diminutive forest denizen was at first thought to represent a hitherto unknown population of the Peruvian antpitta (*Grallaricula peruviana*). But in October 2019 DNA research confirmed it to be a new species, one never before described to science: the latest addition to Colombia's prolific catalogue of avifauna.

Antpittas (Grallariidae family) are small passerine birds unique to the Neotropics. Most are specialized ant-eaters and live on the dark, humid forest floor, where they hop about like thrushes in search of their staple food. Short-tailed, upright and long-legged, they take the name 'pitta' from their resemblance to the Old World birds (Pittidae) of that name, but are much less colourful, being clad largely in subdued browns and ochres.

At just 8 centimetres (a little over 3 in) in length, this is one of the smallest antpitta species. Its name comes from the bobbing, rotating display it performs on a low branch – a party trick it shares with other antpittas. Timid and camouflaged, it is hard to locate unless its thin, whistled call gives it away. Seen well, however, it reveals fine black patterning on the breast and white markings on the face. Like most antpittas, it nests in a tree, where females lay a clutch of one to six eggs.

Our knowledge of the Tororoi bailador is still in its infancy. Scientists from Icesi University, in the city of Cali, are on the case, and a full scientific paper is awaited. Now that the bird's existence has been established, they can investigate its natural history and distribution. Meanwhile, this tiny bird's discovery has reminded us of something significant: that the great forests of the Amazon basin have plenty more secrets to reveal, and that unless those forests are preserved, we may never discover what those secrets are.

Harpy Eagle

Harpia harpyja

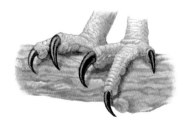

A single swaying cecropia tree is the only evidence of the bloody drama that has just erupted in the treetops of Darién National Park, Panama. There was no struggle; the sloth was dead before it even left the branch, its skull crushed on impact. Now the killer flies back towards its nest in a kapok tree, 3 kilometres (almost 2 miles) away, lifeless victim dangling from its massive talons.

In Greek mythology, the harpies were spirits with a woman's face and an eagle's body, who transported the dead to Hades. Today the eagle that bears their name is the largest in the Americas and the apex predator of the Neotropical treetops, occupying an equivalent niche to the jaguar on the forest floor below. Among eagles worldwide, its average weight of 6–7 kilograms (13–15½ lb) is topped only by Steller's sea-eagle (see page 80). And those talons are the most formidable of any raptor, with a hallux (hind claw) longer than a tiger's claws, at 13 centimetres (5 in) along the curve, and a grip eight times stronger than a human hand's. Such weaponry, mounted on legs as thick as a human wrist, enables it to kill prey as heavy as itself and carry it all the way back to its nest – if not to Hades.

The harpy eagle inhabits dense lowland tropical rainforest. Its usual hunting strategy is sit-and-wait, perching high in an emergent tree to scan the surrounding canopy, then taking flight to ambush any prey it has located, from sloth and monkey to anteater and iguana. The heavily barred wings are more rounded and proportionally shorter than those of open-country eagles, allowing it greater agility among the branches. Powerful hearing is also vital, this eagle can erect the soft-grey feathers around its face into a disc that, like an owl's, amplifies sound by directing it towards the ears.

Harpy eagles mate for life. A pair will reuse the same nest for many years, typically a large platform of sticks high in the fork of a giant tropical hardwood such as a kapok or Brazil nut. One chick is raised every two or three years. The female generally lays two eggs, but the second is ignored and normally fails to hatch unless the first perishes. Incubation takes some 56 days and is largely the job of the female, although the male puts in occasional shifts between hunting trips. The chick fledges at around six months. The parents continue to feed it for another six to ten months, and five years pass before the youngster reaches breeding maturity.

Today, the IUCN lists this species as Near Threatened, with much of its historical range lost to logging, prospecting and cattle-ranching. Outside the Amazon basin, only Panama still has a viable population, centred largely on the wild forests of the Darién Gap along the Colombian border. Here, conservation has benefited from the ancestral knowledge of the indigenous Emberá-Wounaan community, who have long venerated the harpy eagle, with their shamans using woven masks of the bird's face (see overleaf) in healing rituals. One survey in 2000–6 found a record 25 breeding pairs within its study area. This survey also found that each pair used a smaller average breeding territory than that recorded elsewhere. Scientists attributed this exceptional density not only to the quality of the habitat but also to the status the bird enjoys in the indigenous community.

Ultimately, the harpy eagle is an indicator species. Beneath the symbolic umbrella of its 2-metre (6 ft) wingspan lies the fate of the forest and all its inhabitants, humans included. Wherever the eagle has disappeared across its range, it is because the forest has disappeared, too. In April 2002 this magnificent raptor was declared the national bird of Panama. The challenge now is to ensure the bird survives as long as the emblem.

VENEZUELA

Oilbird

Steatornis caripensis

Guácharo Cave, with its 10 kilometres (6¼ miles) of underground chambers and limestone grottos, seemed a fitting choice when in 1977 it was designated Venezuela's first national monument. To ornithologists, however, this landmark in the north of Monagas province is known not so much for its geology as for the bird after which it is named.

Guácharo is the local name for the oilbird, a remarkable nocturnal species that inhabits the cave in its thousands. The bird was first described to science by the German explorer Alexander von Humboldt, who visited in 1799. In the scientific binomial he assigned it, *caripensis* derives from Caripe, the nearest town, while *Steatornis* means 'fat bird' and refers to the plumpness of its chicks. Once harvested for their rendered fat, it is these youngsters that explain the English name 'oilbird'. In nearby Trinidad, the bird is known as *diablotin*, 'little devil', in reference to its screaming calls, which are said to suggest somebody being tortured.

Whatever its name, this is a highly unusual bird. Roughly crow-sized, it has large eyes, a long tail and white-spotted brown plumage that all resemble those of a nightjar, and scientists were quick to place it alongside nightjars in the order Caprimulgiformes. It differs in its larger size and hooked bill, however, plus some unique traits that are enough to make it the sole member of its own family, the Steatornithidae.

Oilbirds roost in caves by day and feed in the forest by night. They have risen to this challenge with some impressive adaptations. Their large pupils are the most light-sensitive of any bird, with millions of tiny rods (the photo-receptor cells) packed together in a tiered arrangement similar to that of some deep-sea fish. What's more, they have echolocation: like bats, oilbirds can navigate around the gloom of their roosting caves by emitting a continuous stream of high-pitched noise that bounces back from the walls – although, unlike those of bats, these noises are audible to us. The only other birds that can do this are the cave-dwelling swiftlets (*Collocalia* species) of South East Asia.

The oilbird's diet of fruit is also unique among nocturnal birds, and it uses a keen sense of smell – again, unusual in birds – to help it sniff out the ripe figs and palm nuts on which it feeds. It plucks this food in flight, using its long wings to hover around the tree canopy, and rictal bristles (fine, whisker-like feathers) around the bill as feelers. Some individuals may forage for more than 100 kilometres (62 miles) in one night, and oilbird droppings play an important role in the dispersal of certain plants.

Oilbirds are monogamous and breed together in large colonies, each pair laying between two and four eggs in a nest of droppings on a rock ledge. Adults feed their nestlings on fruit pulp. This protein-poor diet is unusual for young birds, but baby oilbirds digest their food so slowly that they can eke out every last nutrient, including 80 per cent of the lipids (fats). As a result, they grow huge – at up to 600 grams (21 oz), around 50 per cent larger than their parents. Wise to this resource, local indigenous peoples once collected young oilbirds and boiled down the bodies to render their fat and produce oil for torches.

Outside Venezuela and Trinidad, oilbirds occur in suitable habitat across northern South America, including in Colombia, Peru, Bolivia, Ecuador and Guyana. Preferring forested regions with abundant caves, they will also breed in ravines and canyons, and may roost in trees. Today, no longer harvested, oilbirds are listed by the IUCN as Least Concern – although disturbance to their breeding caves has caused a decline in some regions.

Scarlet Ibis

Eudocimus ruber

No bird does red quite like the scarlet ibis. A flock taking flight against the lush backdrop of Trinidad's Caroni Swamp is a pot of vermilion paint sloshed across an emerald canvas. Perched among the mangroves, the birds are luminous baubles on a Christmas tree. The colour is so bright, so unsubtle, so *scarlet*, it must surely be synthetic.

And yet the outrageous tones of the scarlet ibis are, of course, completely natural, produced – like those of flamingos – by the carotenoid pigments in its diet. These long-legged wading birds feed on tiny crabs and other small crustaceans, probing with their long, decurved bills into the muddy margins of the tropical swamps and shorelines where they make their home. The vivid coloration covers the whole bird except for the wingtips, which are black. Juveniles are a mixture of grey, brown and white, gradually increasing and intensifying through successive moults until, by year two, they have acquired their full scarlet glory.

The breeding range of the scarlet ibis extends around the coastline of northern South America, from Colombia east to Brazil. But it is perhaps in Trinidad, where this species is the national bird, that it is best known, featuring on the coat of arms of Trinidad and Tobago (alongside Tobago's *cocrico* – or rufous-vented chachalaca) and forming large breeding colonies, several thousand strong, that have become a significant tourist draw.

But is the scarlet ibis a species at all? Some taxonomists contend that this bird is merely a variant colour form of the American white ibis (*E. albus*). It's true that the two birds are identical in every respect but their pigmentation. In some areas, such as Venezuela's Llanos wetlands, they even hybridize, with mixed pairs producing pale-orange offspring. By and large, however, the two birds have kept to their separate breeding communities.

Whatever the taxonomic truth, the scarlet ibis's vivid colours once attracted the wrong kind of attention on Trinidad, where the bird was traditionally prized both as aphrodisiac and delicacy – reputedly best served in a spicy curry, as the latter. Hunters would wave pieces of red fabric in the mangroves to lure the birds into range. Today the ibis receives special protection as an 'environmentally sensitive species', and poachers are subject to heavy fines, prison sentences and the ignominy of having slaughtered a national icon. Numbers have recovered, and the population in Caroni Swamp alone is now thought to number up to 30,000.

Rufous Hornero

Furnarius rufus

Some birds' nests are celebrated for their size; others for their intricacy. The rufous hornero's nest is all about strength. This smallish, rather plain-looking songbird uses mud to construct a thick-walled clay dome that bakes hard in the sun to resemble a miniature wood-fired oven, and can last for years. Indeed, the bird gets its name from *horno*, the Spanish for oven, and is also known in English as the red ovenbird.

The nests of rufous horneros, active or abandoned, are a common sight on the savannahs and pastures of central South America, from southern Brazil to northern Patagonia. This is a synanthropic species, having actively benefited from human modifications to the environment, and today it often nests around farmland and settlements – typically on fence posts, outhouses or low branches.

Rufous horneros are monogamous and generally mate for life. A pair tends to build a new nest every year, often beside or even on top of the previous year's. Courtship and territorial displays involve a spirited duet, in which both partners utter a loud trilling call while fluttering their wings in synchronized rhythm. One bird will perch on top of the nest, pointing a beakful of mud skyward, while the other stands in the entrance.

Nest-building may take as little as five days at the start of the breeding season, but modifications and running repairs continue throughout the year. The finished structure is up to 30 centimetres (12 in) wide and 25 centimetres (10 in) high, with walls 3–5 centimetres (1–2 in) thick. Inside, a mud partition separates the entrance from the nest chamber – and there may be an additional entrance at the back.

A female rufous hornero lays two to four eggs, which hatch after 14–18 days. The parents share the work of incubating the clutch and feeding the nestlings, and the thick walls of the domed fortress offer such excellent insulation that they are freed up to take more time foraging for food outside. They are also vigorous in defence against territorial rivals and threats such as snakes, although an unguarded nest may be targeted by the shiny cowbird (*Molothrus bonariensis*), a brood parasite, which will slip in to add its own egg to the clutch. The chicks fledge after 23–26 days, and may remain with their parents to help with nest-building the following year.

Away from its nest, this appears an unremarkable little bird. Starling sized, with rich brown upperparts and a pale throat, it feeds largely on the ground, using its sharp, slightly curved bill to capture insects, spiders and other small arthropods. A member of the large Furnariidae family, indigenous to South and Central America, it should not be confused with the North American ovenbird (*Seiurus aurocapilla*), a migratory warbler of the Parulidae family, whose nest is also oven-shaped, but woven from vegetation.

Today the rufous hornero is listed as Least Concern, an abundant species throughout its range. Its close associations with people – and perhaps the domestic virtues suggested by that nest – have made it a popular character around the homestead. They explain its adoption as a national bird in both Argentina and Uruguay.

MYANMAR

Gurney's Pitta

Hydrornis gurneyi

G urney's pitta is currently enjoying a second life. For 33 years this exquisite little songbird of the damp, tropical forest floor was feared extinct. It was once widespread in Thailand, but no sightings had been recorded since 1952. Then, in 1986, a national survey rediscovered the species in five new sites around the country. Hurrah! Cue wild celebrations among ornithologists.

The celebrations, sadly, were short-lived. By 1997 deforestation had claimed all but one of those sites. Conservationists, believing that just nine pairs remained, declared Gurney's pitta to be the rarest bird in the world. So it was on the way out again – until 2003, when it was found alive and well in Tanintharyi, a southern region of neighbouring Myanmar. Extrapolations for similar habitat elsewhere produced a more optimistic estimate of over 5,000 pairs worldwide. Conservation breathed a cautious sigh of relief. But this rollercoaster story wasn't over yet.

You might wonder how this dazzling little bird could escape detection for so long, with its jet-black and lemon-yellow plumage set off by a crown and tail of electric blue. Like all its kind, however, Gurney's pitta is a shy skulker that vanishes among the shadows of the forest floor, where it searches for earthworms and other small invertebrate prey. Only by playing recordings of its simple territorial chirrup could researchers lure the birds into responding and then track them down.

Gurney's pitta is one of 42 species of pitta, and takes its name from John Henry Gurney (1819–1890), an English politician and amateur ornithologist. The pitta family (Pittidae) belongs to the Passeriformes order and is confined to tropical forest habitats in Africa, Asia and Australasia. This species embodies the family nickname 'jewel-thrush', with its brilliant plumage and upright, long-legged posture – an adaptation to foraging on the forest floor. Pairs are monogamous. They build their large, domed nest in low vegetation, and the female lays up to six eggs.

Unfortunately, the challenges for Gurney's pitta are not over. Like other pittas, this species was once targeted by the cage-bird trade; indeed, information from illegal dealers helped in its rediscovery in Thailand. Now the main threat is deforestation. Since its rediscovery in Myanmar, much of the bird's remaining forest has been lost to oil-palm and betel-nut

154

plantations, and the species is thought to have declined by up to 70 per cent. Civil unrest in the Tanintharyi region has not helped.

Today the IUCN lists Gurney's pitta as Critically Endangered. Conservationists are struggling to shore up its remaining hiding places, which also offer vital refuge for other threatened animals, including the Sunda pangolin (*Manis javanica*) and the Malay tapir (*Tapirus indicus*). Protecting this species isn't easy. It requires arduous treks through dense forest in order to find the birds and, in some cases, fit them with tiny GPS transmitters to monitor their movements. The support of the indigenous Karen community, also engaged in a struggle for autonomy over their ancestral lands, may prove crucial to the species' continued existence.

Helmeted Hornbill

Rhinoplax vigil

The call sounds more ape than bird. At first just soft, sporadic hoots welling up discreetly from the canopy. Then a gradual crescendo, the hoots gaining speed, rhythm and volume as they take over the forest soundscape. Finally, an explosive cackle rings out over the treetops, as though deriding the listener.

A window in the foliage allows a glimpse of the bird behind the noise – and it's an impressive one. At up to 1.7 metres (5½ ft), including its 50-centimetre-long (20 in) central tail plumes, the helmeted hornbill is the longest of the world's hornbills, trumped in weight only by Africa's ground hornbills (*Bucorvus* species). It also sports an extraordinary head, with a wrinkled throat of naked red skin (turquoise in females) and a massive bright-red-and-yellow bill surmounted by an imposing casque – the 'horn' – of keratin.

It is small wonder that a bird so charismatic should have made an impression on the people who share its forests. To the indigenous Punan Bah community of Borneo, this bird is the guardian of the river between life and death. On a lighter note, local folklore also tells how the call mimics the action of a disgruntled young man chopping down his mother-in-law's house, the rhythmic hoots being the blows of his axe on the stilt legs and the manic laughter his hilarity as the house slides down the riverbank and floats off downstream.

Sadly, the helmeted hornbill may not last as long as the folklore it has inspired. The species is disappearing fast, largely because of its bill. In most hornbills, the casque is hollow, serving to amplify the bird's loud territorial calls. The helmeted hornbill's, however, is solid keratin, and bill and casque together make up 10 per cent of the bird's weight. Males use this weaponry in aerial jousts over access to prime treetop real estate, the blows of their clashing casques audible from 100 metres (330 ft) away.

Unfortunately, a solid casque makes a perfect material for carving. For centuries people have hunted this species for its 'hornbill ivory', used to fashion ornaments. In recent decades, however, a formerly small-scale, sustainable harvest has exploded into wholesale commercial slaughter, fuelled by the Chinese market, where a single casque fetches up to US$1,000. In 2012–13 an estimated 6,000 birds were killed, their horns trafficked alongside pangolin scales, tiger teeth and other illegal wildlife products. The scale of the slaughter took conservation authorities by surprise, and in 2015 the bird was upgraded from Near Threatened to Critically Endangered, leapfrogging two rungs on the conservation status ladder overnight.

Helmeted hornbills breed only in remote primary forest, choosing large, old trees. There they undergo the strange breeding ritual peculiar to hornbills, in which the female seals herself inside the nest hole using a plug of mud, fruit and droppings, leaving just a tiny slit through which the male feeds her. She spends the whole incubation period incarcerated, completing a full moult in the process, and breaking out only when the chicks grow too big for the nest. It is during this period, with female and chicks trapped inside and male in constant attendance, that the birds are easy targets.

The helmeted hornbill's natural range extends from Indonesia, where it is confined to Borneo and Sumatra, northwards into the Malay Peninsula. Today, however, it is in steep decline everywhere and extinct in some areas, such as Singapore, where it was once abundant. In 2018 BirdLife International launched a global rescue plan, aiming to halt the illegal trade and to protect the birds' remaining habitat from the relentless march of palm-oil plantations. Rangers now patrol forest trails in prime habitat, and provide special nest boxes if suitable tree holes are in short supply. The bird may yet burst into manic laughter at these efforts. If so, it can only be a good sign.

Sri Lanka Blue Magpie

Urocissa ornata

Magpies come in many guises. This species, which belongs to the *Urocissa* genus of oriental magpies, is not so different in silhouette from the black-and-white magpie of Europe and North America, with its long tail, robust bill and bold, hopping stance. Bring colour into the equation, however, and the similarities cease. Its plumage is a gorgeous combination of dazzling blue and rich chestnut, offset by scarlet bill, legs and eye-ring, and stylish white scalloping beneath the tail. In short, this magpie is a stunner.

The Sri Lanka blue magpie is endemic to Sri Lanka, where it is known in Sinhalese as *kehibella* and has become a popular emblem for the island's unique wildlife, featuring on postage stamps and other cultural artefacts. Its home is the forests in the hilly south, and although it avoids human settlements, requiring undisturbed forest for breeding, it appears to be drawn to the people it encounters in its habitat, showing the habitual curiosity of all corvids when scavenging for handouts.

Like most magpies, this species is omnivorous, feeding on insects, frogs, fruit and other birds' eggs. Small parties forage on the forest floor and mid-canopy, using strong feet to overturn leaf litter and cling acrobatically beneath branches. These foraging parties are highly vocal. Scientists have identified at least 13 common calls, which vary from clicking and chattering to the mimicry of other species. They may even imitate the call of raptors such as the crested serpent eagle (*Spilornis cheela*) while mobbing them, sending out an alarm for other birds that share their patch of forest.

Sri Lanka blue magpies form monogamous pairs and build their neat, cup-shaped nests in tall, slender trees. A female lays three to five eggs and is responsible for incubation. Her mate joins her in feeding the brood, and in this task the pair generally receive help from the previous year's chicks. This strategy, in which youngsters postpone their own breeding ambitions to assist their parents, is known as co-operative breeding. It explains why the species is often seen foraging in small bands of six or seven birds.

Today the Sri Lanka blue magpie is listed as Vulnerable, its estimated population of some 10,000–19,000 individuals (in 2006) at risk from the destruction of native forests. With such environmental pressures unlikely to ease, this dapper bird will need all the ingenuity of its kind to adapt to whatever challenges the future holds.

Red Junglefowl

Gallus gallus

The domestic chicken is, by a distance, the world's most numerous bird. In 2018 the total population stood at an estimated 23.7 billion – that's three chickens for every human. You could argue, in Darwinian terms, that this represents an evolutionary victory for *Gallus gallus*, the species to which it belongs. But given that this victory has been engineered by humankind, and most of the bird's population languishes in abject confinement, it is surely something of a Pyrrhic one.

Either way, the domestic chicken's worldwide proliferation means little to the red junglefowl, its wild ancestor. This handsome gamebird, native to the forests of southern Asia, might attract more admiration were it not for our familiarity with its farmyard descendant. The male is the classic pin-up rooster, decked out in stunning red, orange and metallic green, with a cape of golden hackles and a bustle of dark tail plumes that flash purple in sunlight. Both sexes have the red wattle and comb, but these are more prominent in the male, which, at 1–1.5 kilograms (2¼–3¼ lb), is bigger than his mate – though not as big as the average supermarket chicken.

Archaeology and genetics have revealed that the red junglefowl was domesticated at least 8,000 years ago, probably somewhere in the region of present-day Thailand, with further such events happening in waves across southern Asia. By 5,000 years ago, the bird had reached the South Pacific; by 3,000 years ago, Europe; and by 1,000 years ago, the Americas. It was not until Hellenic times (400–200 BC), however, that the bird was kept for meat and eggs. Until then, its main role had been to provide entertainment and prize money through the brutal sport of cock-fighting – the males set against each other to battle it out using their lethal leg spurs.

The domestic chicken is classified as *G. g. domesticus*, a subspecies of the red junglefowl, with which it shares 71–79 per cent of its DNA. Genome sequencing has revealed traits of other wild ancestors in its genetic mix: the yellow skin, for example, is inherited from the grey junglefowl (*G. sonneratii*) of India. Captive breeding has since produced many breeds in varying shapes and sizes, from Rhode Island Reds to Jersey Giants, but all hail from the same ancestral stock.

The red junglefowl, meanwhile, ranges as a wild bird from the Indian subcontinent through southeastern Asia to the Philippines. It forages around forest edges for seeds – notably those of bamboo – and small invertebrates, and remains shy of humans. Although most of its life is spent on the ground, where its strong legs allow it to flee quickly into the undergrowth, it will take flight when pressed, and habitually roosts in trees. Flocks observe 'pecking orders' similar to those of any chicken coop, and during the breeding season the dominant male's *cock-a-doodle-do* provides a forest wake-up alarm like that of the farmyard rooster. Males court females with solicitous clucking and gifts of food in displays known as 'tidbitting'. No more than 18 eggs are laid per year, with chicks fledging at four or five weeks and reaching sexual maturity at five months.

It is hard to quantify the enormous impact the humble chicken has had on human culture, from the Hindu cremation ceremony to the Chicken McNugget. Some 34 million eggs are consumed daily in the United Kingdom alone, and there is barely a village in the world, from Arctic to Amazon, without at least a few of these birds scratching around its backyards. It is easy to forget, however, that this universal resource arose from a beautiful wild bird, perfectly adapted to fight, forage and flash its finery in the dark forests where it evolved.

Greater Racket-tailed Drongo

Dicrurus paradiseus

To most Australians, 'drongo' means 'idiot' – an affectionate insult dating from the 1920s, when a racehorse of that name reputedly lost all its races. Observe a real drongo, however, and you might question the aptness of the epithet. This alert, intelligent bird has an uncanny ability to manipulate other species to serve its own ends. Indeed, were a drongo to enter a race, you suspect it would win by persuading its competitors to run in the opposite direction.

The greater racket-tailed drongo is arguably the most striking of 29 drongo species that make up the Dicruridae family worldwide. It ranges across the Indian subcontinent and east as far as Borneo, occurring in 13 different geographical subspecies. The size of a starling, it has all-black plumage that gleams with a glossy metallic sheen in sunlight and is set off by a back-curled crest above the base of the bill and two spectacularly long outer-tail feathers, tipped with the tufted 'rackets' that give the bird its name. In flight, these trailing pennants jiggle on barely visible wires, resembling two large, angry black bees in hot pursuit. A robust, hook-tipped bill and piercing red-brown eye give the face a somewhat rapacious expression.

Like all drongos, this is a noisy, active and conspicuous bird. Typically perching somewhere high and prominent, near the forest edge, it keeps up a wide range of calls from dawn to dusk, including clicks, whistles and various metallic and nasal sounds. Indeed, in parts of India its upright demeanour and piercing whistle have earned it the folk name *kothwal*, meaning guard or policeman.

This vocal repertoire extends to mimicking other bird species. Unlike most avian mimics, however, the drongo does not simply borrow other voices to improve its own, but may actively use them to mislead their real owners. When a mixed flock of small birds gathers at a rich feeding source, for example, the drongo tags along, mimicking their calls to recruit more members to the flock, thus benefiting from the other birds' spadework as they reveal food it can grab for itself. To distract its fellow flockers, it may even mimic the call of a raptor, such as a shikra (*Accipiter badius*), sending them into a panic and allowing it to swoop down and pinch their prize.

The drongo's diet ranges from insects to fruit and nectar. It defends its food sources fiercely, diving at larger birds to drive them away, and may turn this aggression on birds such as woodpeckers in order to pirate their food. Equally, it often follows behind larger animals, such as monkeys, to take advantage of leftovers from their foraging.

Greater racket-tailed drongos are commonly seen in their monogamous pairs, but may also form small, loose groups. During the breeding season, males perform acrobatic courtship displays, hopping and turning on a branch, and flying up to drop objects before catching them in mid-air, the tail rackets producing an audible hum as the bird twists and turns. A female lays her three or four eggs in a cup-shaped nest in a tree fork. The youngsters may remain with their parents for a season, helping to rear the next brood of chicks while picking up those special drongo tricks of the trade.

Brahminy Kite

Haliastur indus

The origins of this bird's name are unclear. In India's Hindu traditions, brahmins were priests and teachers, officiating in ceremonies and occupying the highest rank in the ancient caste system. One suggestion, based on social prejudice surrounding skin colour, holds that the bird owes its lofty status to its white-plumaged head; this argument is supported by the fact that its darker-plumaged cousin the black kite (*Milvus migrans*) was traditionally known as the 'pariah kite'.

Whatever the explanation, the brahminy kite is celebrated in Hindu scripture and mythology as the modern representation of Garuda, the sacred mount of the god Vishnu and traditionally depicted with red or golden wings and an eagle's beak – all recognizable traits of this raptor. In Tamil, the bird is known as *Krishna parunthu*, Krishna also being an avatar of Vishnu. This cultural importance extends further east: to the Iban community of Upper Rajang, Sarawak, the brahminy kite is the manifestation of the ultimate deity, Singalang Burong; in Singapore, tradition holds that the bird's presence provides guidance in difficult decisions, from architecture to warfare; and in Indonesia, it is the mascot of the capital city, Jakarta.

Given these illustrious cultural associations, the less than glorious truth about this bird – that it is largely a scavenger, and often steals food from other species – may come as a disappointment. Nonetheless, the brahminy kite is certainly a handsome species and well suited to iconography, in its attractive livery of reddish brown, with striking white head and breast, and smart black wingtips. This makes it a conspicuous sight in the wetlands where it lives, both along the coast and inland, cruising in buoyant flight on the lookout for dead fish and crabs, and periodically swooping to snatch prey from the water's surface.

The brahminy kite ranges widely through the region, from the Indian subcontinent east through South East Asia as far as Australia. In this last haunt, it is also known as the red-backed sea-eagle. This species is smaller than most eagles, however, with a wingspan of no more than 1.2 metres (4 ft). Together with the whistling kite (*H. sphenurus*) of Australia, it makes up the kite genus *Haliastur*, both distinguished from the more typical *Milvus* kites by their square-ended rather than forked tails.

In India, this species breeds between December and April. Monogamous pairs build their stick nest in a tree, typically a mangrove, returning to the same site every year. The female lays two eggs and the young fledge at six weeks but do not reach sexual maturity for another two years. Juveniles enjoy larking about, often dropping and catching large leaves in mid-air. Adults will also readily mob larger raptors – although this can prove their undoing, as steppe eagles (*Aquila nipalensis*) occasionally kill brahminy kites. It seems even the sacred emissary of Vishnu is not always guaranteed protection.

Common Tailorbird

Orthotomus sutorius

'Nag is dead – is dead – is dead!' So sings Darzee the tailorbird in 'Rikki-Tikki-Tavi' from Rudyard Kipling's *The Jungle Book*. In this celebrated tale, Nag is a cobra threatening a family, Rikki-Tikki-Tavi is a mongoose who lives in their garden, and the bird is celebrating the latter's heroics in helping the father kill the deadly snake. The drama doesn't end there, however, as Nagaina, Nag's wife, swears revenge. But Darzee's wife feigns injury, distracting the snake long enough for Rikki-Tikki-Tavi to steal her eggs. In the final showdown, the mongoose has the last word, killing Nagaina and saving the family.

Tailorbirds inhabit parks, gardens and similar spaces across much of southern and southeastern Asia. Small birds, with a green back, chestnut crown and long, jauntily cocked tail, they attract attention with their loud, repetitive calls. Kipling got that much right. He was wrong about feigning injury, though: this 'distraction display' technique *is* known from plovers but not from warblers, of which the tailorbird is one.

The common tailorbird is the most widespread of 13 similar species that make up the *Orthotomus* genus. The group derives its common name from the ingenious nest-building technique shared by many. Using its fine bill, the bird punches tiny holes around the margin of a large leaf and draws through fine strands of spider silk or plant fibre – just like a tailor using needle and thread. *Darzee*, Kipling's character, is the Urdu word for tailor, although the bird's scientific species name, *sutorius*, actually means 'cobbler'.

In fact, tailorbirds do not quite create a series of stitches, but rather use the fibrous thread as rivets, folding and fastening the leaf into a cradle, inside which they build a snug nest using soft materials such as the lint from euphorbias. In India, breeding peaks between June and August. A female lays three eggs, which she incubates for 12 days. After fledging, the youngsters may roost with their parents, sandwiched tightly together on a thin twig.

Like all warblers, tailorbirds are insectivores, foraging for their food in low vegetation or on the ground. They are often drawn to flowers – chiefly in order to snap up the insects also attracted to the blooms, although they may also take some nectar themselves. With hawks and snakes lurking in the undergrowth, the birds are quick to sound the alarm. Only in Kipling, however, do they receive a helping hand from a mongoose.

Sarus Crane

Antigone antigone

Picture the scene. Deep in the green, watery wilderness of Cambodia's Mekong Delta, fishermen cast their nets from wooden dugouts while women sift rice from panniers beside their palm-thatched stilt houses. It seems a timeless tableau. But any timelessness is an illusion. Today the delta is under increasing pressure from a growing local population, and some 70 million people in six countries depend on the resources of the Mekong basin. In the last 15 years alone, around half this rich natural wetland has been lost to agriculture and development, and its wildlife has suffered accordingly – not least the world's tallest flying bird.

The sarus crane towers up to 1.8 metres (6 ft) in height. Uniform grey in plumage, topped by a naked red head and upper neck, it is an impressive and unmistakable sight – especially during its leaping and bowing courtship display, which, like those of many cranes, is performed to a spirited bugling accompaniment. With its omnivorous diet encompassing seeds, invertebrates and small animals such as frogs, sarus cranes find plentiful food among the ditches and swamps of the traditional south Asian agricultural landscape, where canals and paddy fields provide excellent habitat.

Every rainy season, after renewing their monogamous lifelong bonds in flamboyant displays, pairs choose a hidden wetland site in which to produce the next generation. The nest is a circular mound of vegetation up to 2 metres (6½ ft) across and 1 metre (3 ft) high. There the parents take turns to incubate their brood of one or two eggs, which hatch after an average of 31 days. They are aggressive in defending their chicks against natural predators, such as foxes or crows, but the presence of wandering humans can tip the balance from breeding success to failure. Studies from Cambodia reveal that under unprotected conditions, only 30 per cent of breeding pairs are successful.

Today, Cambodia has the highest population of sarus cranes in southeastern Asia, with around 1,000 individuals. Once common across the region, the species suffered from decades of conflict in the late twentieth century and subsequent agricultural intensification. It is now extirpated from Malaysia and the Philippines, and small numbers occur in Laos, Vietnam and Myanmar. Elsewhere, the species exists in two separate subspecies: one in northeastern Australia; and one in India, which now holds the bulk of the world's population. Indeed, it is from India that the species derives its name – *sarasa* being Sanskrit for 'lake bird'.

Across its range, the sarus crane has long been emblematic of marital fidelity. It is said in India, where the species is venerated as sacred, that the bird will pine away if its partner dies. In Cambodia, this popularity is proving important in the species' conservation. Since the launch of the Sarus Crane Conservation Project in 2006, local communities have learned how to live alongside cranes by managing natural resources more sustainably. Meanwhile, local guardians are employed to protect breeding pairs – increasing breeding success rates in some regions to an impressive 87 per cent – while a visitor homestay programme is generating tourist revenue. With the sarus crane as a flagship, conservationists are working to protect the remaining remnants of precious wetland, creating new homes for cranes and promoting a sustainable natural environment for all the delta's inhabitants, people and wildlife alike.

Malayan Peacock-pheasant

Polyplectron malacense

Pheasants in general are among the most beautiful of birds, and peacock-pheasants are no exception. But while many pheasants flaunt showy, in-your-face coloration, these denizens of the dark forest floor have a subtler palette. In the shadows, they appear a plain brownish-grey. Seen up close, however, that apparent uniformity reveals an ornate embellishment of spots and bars and, across the upperparts and tail, a sprinkling of dozens of iridescent blue-green eye-spots that flash in the light like mirrors.

As with all gamebirds, only the male boasts this finery. During courtship, he deploys his plumage in an impressive display, fanning his tail feathers peacock-style, but tilting them laterally, while drooping one wing, to change shape into an elliptical shield of mirrors. This performance does not only impress females, but may also deter predators, which are unsure what they are up against – especially when the weird visuals come with an intimidating buzzing sound, as the performer vibrates his tail quills at high speed. As a last resort, fierce kicks from the sharp metatarsal spurs help repel rival and predator alike.

The Malayan peacock-pheasant is one of eight similar peacock-pheasant species that make up the genus *Polyplectron*. Shy and elusive, it inhabits lowland dipterocarp forests, where it forages at ground-level for seeds, fruit and small arthropods. Breeding takes place year-round. The nest is a simple twig-lined scrape on the forest floor, in which the camouflaged female lays just a single egg – a very low return for gamebirds – which she incubates for 22–23 days. Juveniles don't acquire the adult male's finery until they've moved away to find a place of their own.

This once wide-ranging species is now thought to be confined to central Malaysia – notably in protected areas, such as Taman Negara National Park – with possibly a tiny remnant population in southern Thailand. Although long targeted by hunters for both its meat and plumes, the bird's recent decline is largely due to deforestation, with more than 50 per cent of viable habitat lost since the 1970s. Today, with just 7,000 individuals estimated to remain, the IUCN lists the species as Vulnerable. Captive breeders overseas are now working with conservationists in Malaysia on a reintroduction programme; at the time of writing, one female has provided 19 chicks over 25 years for a new life in their wild homeland.

Nicobar Pigeon

Caloenas nicobarica

The Nicobar Islands lie in the Bay of Bengal, part of India's Andaman and Nicobar Islands Union Territory, and are among the world's most remote outposts. With no historical land connection to mainland Asia, their tropical seclusion offers a home to numerous unusual species, including this unique and ancient pigeon.

The Nicobar pigeon is unmistakable, its head and neck draped in a necklace of metallic-green plumes called hackles that gleam copper in sunlight. At 600 grams (21 oz), this is one of the world's largest pigeons. However, it was once dwarfed by the largest pigeon ever known, the 15 kilogram (33 lb) dodo. That big flightless bird was a fellow Indian Ocean islander, endemic to Mauritius, before rats and sailors brought about its demise. Scientists believe that the Nicobar pigeon may now be the dodo's closest living relative, both birds having evolved from an island line that split away from other birds during the Eocene epoch (56–33.9 million years ago) and also produced the now equally extinct Rodrigues solitaire.

Like those long-gone cousins, the Nicobar pigeon is primarily a ground-feeder, searching the forest floor for seeds, fruit and grain, which it grinds down using a gizzard stone. Unlike them, however, it is perfectly capable of flight. Indeed, flying is integral to a lifestyle that involves feeding on large, food-rich islands by day then retreating every evening to its roosts on smaller, predator-free islands. Flocks of up to 40 birds wing swiftly across the water, their short white tails providing 'landing lights' that enable them to stick together in the half-light of dusk and dawn.

Breeding takes place in large, loose colonies, also on offshore islets. Females lay a single white egg in a flimsy stick nest and, like all pigeons, parents feed their nestlings on a soup of regurgitated, semi-digested grain called 'pigeon milk'. Juveniles lack their parents' white tails, thus signalling to adult males that they are neither potential adversaries nor mates.

The Nicobar pigeon ranges east from the Nicobar Islands across the Malay Archipelago to Palau in the western Pacific, with the odd wanderer even reaching Western Australia. Numbers are thought to be decreasing, the bird threatened by habitat loss, invasive predators and hunting notably for its gizzard stone, prized in jewellery. The devastating Indian Ocean tsunami of 2004 also took a toll. Today the IUCN lists it as Near Threatened – mindful, perhaps, of the fate of its famous cousin.

Philippine Eagle

Pithecophaga jefferyi

ird books from a bygone era labelled this mighty raptor the
'monkey-eating eagle'. This colourful name came courtesy of the
English naturalist John Whitehead, who, in 1896, sent back the
first known specimen to Europe. When it was shot, the bird's stomach
had contained undigested pieces of monkey. In 1978, by proclamation
of president Ferdinand Marcos, the species received its patriotic but
rather more prosaic new name, and in 1995 it acquired its official status
as national bird of the Philippines. Today, the bird's history lurks in its
scientific name: *Pithecophaga*, the genus of which this species is the only
member, derives from the Greek *pithecus* and *phagus*, meaning 'monkey' and
'eating'; *jefferyi* refers to Whitehead's father.

Sadly, national bird status is no guarantee of security. Today the
Philippine eagle is one of the world's rarest birds, and is listed as Critically
Endangered. Endemic to the Philippines, where it inhabits primary
forest in mountainous areas, it occurs on just four islands, with most of
the population (some 250 breeding pairs at the time of writing) largely
confined to Mindanao, and a few more on Samar, Leyte and Luzon.

This species is one of three that contest the title 'world's biggest
eagle', the others being the harpy eagle (see page 144) and Steller's
sea-eagle (see page 80). At up to 102 centimetres (40 in) it wins in terms
of length, but it falls fractionally behind its rivals in average weight. Still,
this is a formidable bird. Chocolate-brown above and creamy white below,
it has a fierce demeanour that is accentuated by a hatchet bill and a spray
of elongated nape feathers that it can erect in a lion-like mane around
its dark face and piercing pale eyes. A startling resemblance to the harpy
eagle – in size, appearance and forest lifestyle – explains why for years it
was classified in the subfamily Harpiinae. However, molecular research has
since revealed this species to be more closely related to the Circaetinae
snake eagles.

Whatever its name and taxonomy, the Philippine eagle is the most
powerful terrestrial predator on the islands. On Mindanao, its staple prey
is the arboreal, cat-sized Philippine flying lemur (*Cynocephalus volans*). Other
prey ranges from monitor lizards to large birds such as hornbills, taking
in young pigs, small dogs and even, of course, the occasional monkey
specifically the long-tailed macaque (*Macaca fascicularis*). The eagle hunts

by swooping down on prey from a hidden perch or by foraging from branch to branch, generally working downwards through the canopy.

Philippine eagles have an exceptionally slow breeding cycle, raising just one chick every two or three years. Pairs nest on average 13 kilometres (8 miles) apart. Every spring they renew their lifelong bonds with tumbling aerial displays. The large stick nest is built in a tall emergent dipterocarp tree and lined with green leaves. The female invariably lays just one egg. Incubation lasts around 62 days, and for the first seven weeks the parents take turns sheltering the hatchling. The youngster fledges at around five months but will stay with its parents for up to another 18 months, not making its own kills for nearly a year. Birds may live for up to 30 years in the wild, with captive individuals having reached 46.

The decline of this mighty bird comes down to deforestation, which is still rampant in the Philippines. Pollution, pesticides and accidental snaring don't help, while illegal hunting continues – despite prison sentences of up to 12 years for those caught. Conservation began in the 1970s, prompted by the famous US aviator Charles Lindbergh, and today the Philippine Eagle Foundation, based in Davao City, Mindanao, oversees captive-breeding and reintroduction efforts and the conservation of wild populations. Progress is slow. This magnificent bird teeters on the brink.

Southern Cassowary

Casuarius casuarius

A cassowary is hard to mistake for anything else. First, there's its size: approaching 2 metres (6½ ft) tall and weighing 70 kilograms (154 lb) or more, this is the world's second-largest bird after the ostrich (see page 34). Then there's its appearance: a mound of black feathers on two huge legs, surmounted by a naked bright-blue neck with two pendulous scarlet wattles, and a shark's-fin casque on top of its head. 'Living dinosaur' is one popular description. Certainly, this is not most people's idea of a bird.

The southern, or double-wattled, cassowary is the largest of three similar species and the only one found in Australia, the other two being confined to New Guinea and its offshore islands. All belong to the ratite group, which means that – like their cousins, ostriches and kiwis – they are flightless. Leaving aside weight, this trait is evident from their hair-like feathers and the absence of the keeled sternum that, in flying birds, anchors the flight muscles. Instead of flying, a cassowary's powerful legs can propel it through the rainforest tangle at speeds of up to 50 kph (30 mph). Its three-toed feet are equipped with wicked claws, the inner one a 15-centimetre (6 in) dagger. An agitated cassowary can deliver lethal kicks; *Guinness World Records* lists this as 'the most dangerous bird in the world', and human fatalities have been recorded. In reality, attacks are very rare and occur only where this naturally shy creature has been habituated by feeding. Unsurprisingly, such feeding is not encouraged.

That strange casque has prompted much debate. Scientists once thought it served as a crash helmet, protecting the bird's skull against collisions with forest tree trunks, or perhaps as a sexual signal in courtship. More recent theories suggest that its function relates to the bird's booming mating call. This call is the loudest in decibels of any bird, although its low frequency makes it almost inaudible to humans. The casque is formed of a spongy cellular material that, some think, might either help to amplify the call or allow the bird to detect the calls of others – as has also been suggested for dinosaur species such as *Corythosaurus* that sported similar structures.

Breeding is a slow process. A female cassowary lays a clutch of 3–8 large pale-green eggs directly on the forest floor, whereupon she departs and the male takes over. He tends the clutch for around two months, adding or removing leaf litter to maintain the optimum incubation temperature. He then cares for his brood after they hatch, seeing off any predators. The youngsters start life with stripy yellow-brown camouflage outfits, taking two years to moult into their black adult plumage and another year to reach breeding maturity. As adults, they are solitary, except when breeding and tending young. In captivity, individuals have lived for more than 40 years.

In Australia, the population of some 2,000 southern cassowaries is confined to the rainforest of northern Queensland. In New Guinea, the species is more widespread. Threats are numerous throughout its range, from road traffic and hunters to feral pigs that compete for food. Its loss from any location leaves a hole, since cassowaries are a 'keystone' species in rainforest ecology. They feed primarily on fruit, taken from the forest floor or low branches, and their droppings are vital dispersal agents for many trees. Tests have shown that germination rates for several species, including *Ryparosa*, can almost double if their seeds have passed through a cassowary.

Satin Bowerbird

Ptilonorhynchus violaceus

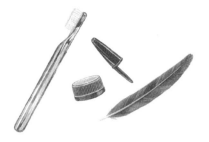

The stage is set: two short, parallel lines of twigs and dry grass stems stuck into the ground, facing each other like empty bookends. Around them, the leaf litter glitters with bright blue. There are blue flowers, blue feathers and the more synthetic blues of clothes pegs, pen lids and bottle tops, all arranged tastefully to enhance the architecture.

This is the work of a male satin bowerbird. While many birds build intricate nests, only bowerbirds create stage sets. These 'bowers' come in two main designs: some species build maypole bowers, with sticks arranged around a sapling; others, including this one, build avenue bowers, with lines of sticks either side of a central passage. Each species has its own preference for interior decor. The satin bowerbird works largely in blue, and suburban populations will use any blue manmade items they can find. Once built, regular adjustments keep the bower in tip-top condition.

Every stage needs a performance, of course. The male has built his bower to impress females, and when one arrives he snaps into his routine, leaping and strutting with quivering wings outstretched, while pouring out a strange mechanical song. Success is not guaranteed. Females visit all males in a neighbourhood to assess the quality of both bower and performance, sometimes checking out the structure when its owner is absent. They then retreat to build a nest before making their final decision.

Studies have shown that young female satin bowerbirds tend to base their choice on the male's bower, while more experienced birds go more by his display. Either way, once a female has chosen a suitor, the birds will mate inside his bower. She then returns to the nest to get laying. Her clutch of two or three eggs hatch after 21 days and fledge after 21 more. The male stays at the bower, hoping for further mates and chasing off rivals who may try to steal or sabotage his designs.

The satin bowerbird is one of 20 different bowerbird species, and inhabits woodlands in eastern coastal Australia, with a separate isolated population in the northern rainforest. The jackdaw-sized male is identified by his glossy blue-black plumage, set off by a silvery bill and violet iris. Females and young are largely olive-green and, unlike males, often occur in small flocks. This species is one of the longest-lived passerines – ringers have documented a record age of 26 years in the wild – and males do not perfect their building technique until the age of seven or eight.

Budgerigar

Melopsittacus undulatus

A green cloud sweeps along the outback horizon, twisting against blue sky and red earth like a gathering tornado. It's a flock of birds – thousands of them. The distant murmur intensifies into a roar as they approach, a whoosh of innumerable wings and cheeping voices, moving with the synchronicity of a single organism.

The popular idea of a budgerigar is of a bird behind bars. After all, this pocket-sized parrot, domesticated in the 1850s, is the third most popular family pet worldwide, treasured for its cheerful voice and showy colours. The largely green plumage of the wild bird has since given rise to new varieties in blue, white, yellow and grey. It is thus easy to forget that this species is naturally native to the arid scrublands of central Australia, where huge nomadic flocks move restlessly in search of food and water.

The budgerigar uses its downward-pointed bill to strip seeds from spinifex, saltbush and other outback plants. Like all seed-eaters, it has to drink regularly. Rainfall in the outback is unpredictable, alternating between drought and downpour, so budgerigars must respond quickly when it appears. Small advance parties scout the terrain and scour the horizon, detecting rainfall from up to 60 kilometres (37 miles) away. Smaller flocks quickly merge into larger ones, up to hundreds of thousands strong.

The budgerigar's ability to find water may explain its name: *betcherrygah* means 'good food' in the language of the Gamilaraay people of central Australia and is thought to refer not to the bird itself but to its capacity to lead the way to water and thus to new growth. Either way, budgerigars are well adapted to survive their harsh environment, and in suitable conditions they form loose breeding colonies, each pair building a nest inside a hole in a tree, fence post or fallen log. A pair may produce several broods a year, so population growth can be explosive.

Budgerigars inhabit much of Australia, being absent only from Tasmania, Cape York and some coastal regions. The wild population fluctuates with conditions. Droughts and bushfires take their toll, as does the replacement of native seed plants by invasive species. Conversely, irrigation schemes and livestock farming have introduced water to once arid regions, allowing the birds to flourish where previously they couldn't. In captivity, meanwhile, the species thrives in its millions, oblivious to the challenges facing its wild ancestors.

Laughing Kookaburra

Dacelo novaeguineae

You needn't have visited Australia to have heard the laugh of the kookaburra. The manic cackle of this outsized kingfisher is the default soundtrack to the jungle adventure movie, from the Johnny Weissmuller classic *Tarzan the Ape Man* to Steven Spielberg's dinosaur thriller *Jurassic Park*. No matter that the bird is Australian, and that these movies were set, respectively, somewhere in Africa and Central America.

To Australians, however, there is nothing especially wild about the kookaburra, which, across much of the country, is perfectly at home in suburbia, finding the same rich pickings in parks and large gardens as it does in its native eucalypt woodland. Its call always raises an eyebrow, however, and can be decidedly alarming to the first-timer. Rising from a throaty chuckle to a ringing *ha-ha-ha* and chimp-like *oo-oo-oo*, one voice may be joined by its companions in a full-throated territorial chorus – sounding wild and other-worldly, especially in the half-light of dawn or dusk.

The bird itself is not as big as its voice might suggest. Nonetheless, this is the largest of the world's kingfishers, the rook-sized males weighing over 400 grams (13½ oz), and – to the animals on which it preys – a deadly predator. Kookaburras are ambush hunters, perching quietly on a branch to scan the ground below, then swooping down to snatch their victim in their heavy, boat-shaped bill. Prey comprises large insects, small mammals and reptiles, and this bird is an expert catcher of snakes, overpowering individuals over 75 centimetres (30 in) long by whip-cracking their head against the ground, then swallowing them whole. Despite being a kingfisher, this bird does not hunt in water.

The laughing kookaburra is the largest of four species in the genus *Dacelo*, with two being confined to New Guinea. 'Kookaburra' is derived from the onomatopoeic *guuguubarra* in the indigenous Wiradjuri language. The etymology of the scientific name is less straightforward. Taxonomists chose *novaeguineae* under the erroneous belief that the first specimen was obtained in New Guinea – courtesy of tall tales from the eighteenth century French explorer Pierre Sonnerat, who had never been near that island. In fact, this species does not occur on New Guinea at all. The genus name *Dacelo* is simply an anagram of *Alcedo*, the genus name of the European kingfisher. To anyone who has heard the bird's call, meanwhile, its nickname 'laughing jackass' feels perfect.

Apart from its size and bill, this species can be identified by its white head with brown eye-stripe, and the panel of blue on its otherwise brown wings. It nests in holes, either in tree trunks or the nests of arboreal termites. Pairs are monogamous and mate for life, the female producing one brood of three eggs each year. The third and youngest chick may be killed in the nest by its bullying siblings. Nonetheless, the remaining youngsters may stay with their parents for a year or more, helping to raise the next brood and joining in the family's territorial defence – hence the cackling chorus. Although naturally confined to eastern Australia, the laughing kookaburra has been introduced to a number of other places, including southwestern Australia and Tasmania, largely in the hope that it would help reduce the number of snakes. A small population was even introduced to New Zealand's Hauraki Gulf in the 1860s. As an emblem, meanwhile, the bird appears across Australian culture – everywhere from children's nursery rhymes to cricket balls and $20 notes.

Kakapo

Strigops habroptila

The first European visitors to New Zealand reported finding kakapos so common that they could shake them out of low trees like apples. Sadly, by the 1970s, hunting, habitat destruction and alien predators had left this unique parrot on the brink of extinction. Today, after five decades of intensive conservation, only about 200 individuals remain. Each is known by its own name.

The kakapo is hardly your typical parrot. Flightless and nocturnal, it has a whiskery, owl-like face, utters an eerie 'boom' in place of a squawk and is as heavy as a cat, with males weighing up to 4 kilograms (nearly 9 lb). These odd traits have their origin in plate tectonics. When New Zealand broke away from Gondwana, 82 million years ago, it left mammals behind, making ground-level a safer place for birds. The kakapo was one of many that adapted to do without flight. It has shorter wings than flying birds, lacks their large pectoral muscles, keeled sternum and fused clavicles, and its soft plumage serves for insulation, not flight. With no need to get airborne, it can also store extra body fat for lean times. The bird has, in effect, evolved to fill an ecological niche occupied elsewhere by mammals.

Kakapos roost by day in dense ground cover, camouflaged by their greenish plumage. At night they feed on native plants, notably the conifer rimu, grinding down seeds in their chunky bill. Unlike many parrots, they do not form pair bonds. Instead, males attract females by trekking on their sturdy feet to a 'mating court' in the hills. There, each competitor scrapes several bowl-like depressions in the ground to amplify his booming calls, uttered by inflating an air sac in his chest. He performs for up to eight hours a night, moving from bowl to bowl. On still nights, the sound draws females from afar.

Once a female has mated, she heads back to start nesting while the male, who plays no part in parenting, continues booming to attract the next in line. Three eggs are laid in a hidden ground nest. The chicks hatch after 30 days and leave the nest at 10–12 weeks, but their mother may continue feeding them for another three months. Kakapos breed on average only once every three years, notably when rimu trees fruit. They are slow to mature, and may live to an impressive 60 years or more.

Humans are responsible for the kakapo's decline. The first to reach New Zealand were the Polynesians, 1,000 years ago. They hunted the bird for its food and feathers, and left it defenceless against their rats and dogs. By the 1840s, the Europeans had arrived, bringing cats, stoats and rampant deforestation. Conservation began in the 1890s, but alien predators ransacked every safe haven and individuals seldom survived in captivity.

By the 1970s, the kakapo was feared extinct. In 1977, however, a small population was discovered on Stewart Island and the Kakapo Recovery Plan soon swung into action. In 1989, all remaining birds were relocated to a handful of offshore islands, where invasive predators had been eradicated and native vegetation restored. Since then, the population has slowly increased and at the time of writing there are 209 individuals, each one tagged, monitored and given an annual health check. More islands are now being prepared in order to establish self-sustaining populations. The bird remains Critically Endangered.

North Island Brown Kiwi

Apteryx mantelli

N o national bird is more closely identified with a nation's people than is New Zealand's flightless oddity, the kiwi. Today, the very word is a universal nickname for New Zealanders themselves, proudly embraced wherever they travel in the world.

'Kiwi' is originally Maori. Opinion divides over whether it is an onomatopoeic transcription of the bird's call or derives from the Polynesian name for bristle-thighed curlew (*Numenius tahitiensis*), a migratory wader whose long, curved bill resembles a kiwi's. Either way, kiwis first appeared on New Zealand regimental insignia during the nineteenth century and the word entered popular usage elsewhere during World War I, when New Zealand soldiers became known as kiwis. It also gained traction in 1906 with the advent of Kiwi shoe polish. The popularity of this household brand has even caused 'kiwi' to become a verb in Malay, meaning to polish one's shoes. Ironically, the brand is Australian.

With its pear-shaped body and tiny wings hidden by hair-like feathers, a kiwi appears almost more mammal than bird. And this perception is not so wide of the mark: with New Zealand having no native terrestrial mammals, kiwis are among several native birds (see kakapo, page 192) that have evolved to fill the vacant ecological niches and in the process lost the power of flight. Today those tiny wings are all but useless. Indeed, the scientific genus name *Apteryx* means 'without wing'.

Taxonomically, kiwis are the smallest of an assemblage of flightless birds worldwide known as ratites. The North Island brown kiwi is the most numerous of five species. Like the others, it is largely nocturnal – although it may have been less so before humans showed up. With poor eyesight, it relies on its long, highly sensitive bill to locate worms and insects in the forest leaf litter. Kiwis are unique among birds in having nostrils at the bill's tip, giving them the strongest sense of smell in the bird world.

Kiwi pair bonds are monogamous and lifelong. During courtship, the birds call by night then meet in their burrows by day. Once mated, the female produces, proportionally, the bird world's biggest egg – taking up to 20 per cent of her own weight. It takes 30 days to develop and places huge demands on her, obliging her to fast for the last days before laying, as there is no space left for her stomach, and even to squat in puddles to relieve the strain. This species is the only kiwi that may produce two eggs, the second laid 25 days after the first. Incubation is the responsibility of the male and lasts 63–92 days. The chicks hatch ready to go and leave their burrows after ten days, with no parent in sight.

New Zealand's kiwi species are all now listed by the IUCN as either Vulnerable or Near Threatened. Their fortunes plummeted the moment humans reached the islands, with introduced mammals – including dogs, stoats and wild pigs – finding their eggs and hatchlings easy prey. Today only 5–10 per cent of chicks would survive to adulthood without invasive predator control. Nonetheless, the North Island brown kiwi – the only species that occurs naturally on North Island – has shown enough versatility to adapt from its native forests to survive on farmland and plantations. Its population is estimated at 30,000.

Superb Bird-of-paradise

Lophorina superba

A damp forest floor in the mountains of Papua New Guinea is the setting for an extraordinary dance routine. Prompted by the arrival of a female, a male superb bird-of-paradise hops forward and erects his breast shield, a triangle of iridescent blue. Next, he fans his nape plumes into a jet-black cape that he flourishes over his back in a perfect ellipse. Then he bows his head, making his face vanish and exposing two bright crown spots that glow like eyes against the blackness. At last, costume in place, he starts to dance, bouncing around the female and snapping his tail feathers together with a sound like clicking fingers. By mid-display, it is hard to believe that this bizarre apparition is a bird at all.

When the first European explorers encountered bird-of-paradise skins, they were told by the locals that these birds had no legs but float around the heavens, living on dew, until eventually they fall to Earth. For more than 150 years this myth persisted, giving rise to the birds' name. After all, the explorers reasoned, such extraordinary plumes must surely belong to something that was not of this world. In fact, the legs had simply been removed. Today we know that birds-of-paradise – of which there are some 50 species, all restricted to New Guinea and its satellite islands, with a few in eastern Australia – are a perfectly mortal family of birds loosely related to crows. Strip away the fancy plumes and you'll see they have normal bird shapes beneath, and range in size from starling to pigeon.

It is the plumage of breeding males that causes the fuss. Most species sport extravagant ornamentation, from the cascading golden flank plumes of the greater bird-of-paradise to the spiral-coiled tail wires of Wilson's bird-of-paradise. The idea is to impress a mate. Most species are polygynous, each male mating with several females. Some display together in a competitive lek. Others, including the superb bird-of-paradise, display in individual 'courts', prepared by stripping foliage or sweeping away leaves. Every species has a unique combination of colours, dance and song. Competition is intense; a male superb bird-of-paradise performs for many hours a day and the average female rejects 15–20 suitors before choosing Mr Right.

The superb bird-of-paradise inhabits forest in New Guinea's central mountains at an altitude of 1,000–2,300 metres (3,300–7,500 ft). It feeds on fruit and arthropods in the tree canopy and on the ground. The female – which, as in all species, is much drabber than her partner – performs all parenting duties. She makes a nest of leaves, ferns and other soft plant materials in a tree fork, in which she lays one to three eggs. Incubation lasts 16–22 days and the young fledge after another 18 days. Males can take four years to develop display plumage, although females can breed after two.

Bird-of-paradise plumes and skins have featured in New Guinea dress and ritual for millennia, and have been traded in Asia for at least 2,000 years. The first seen in the West were a gift to the Portuguese explorer Ferdinand Magellan from the Sultan of Batchian (Bacan) in the sixteenth century. The plumes became fashionable during the nineteenth century, and 155,000 skins were sold in London alone in 1904–8. In 1922 the feather trade was banned, and today hunting is illegal, except for a sustainable quota used in traditional culture. Habitat destruction poses a more serious threat, although this species remains abundant and is listed by the IUCN as Least Concern.

Emperor Penguin

Aptenodytes forsteri

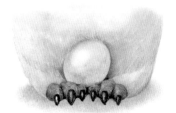

The vaults of London's Natural History Museum house three emperor penguin eggs collected from Antarctica by the English explorer Apsley Cherry-Garrard. Few items in the museum's collection can have been more difficult to obtain. Cherry-Garrard was assistant zoologist on Robert Falcon Scott's ill-fated expedition to the South Pole in 1911. To collect the eggs, he and two companions hiked 100 kilometres (62 miles) across Ross Island, enduring temperatures of -60°C (-76°F) and a Force 11 blizzard that destroyed both their tent and the igloo they subsequently built, obliging them to sleep in the open. Cherry-Garrard lost most of his teeth through the violence of their chattering. He thus knew what he was talking about when, in his account of the expedition, he wrote: 'I do not believe anybody on earth has a worse time than an Emperor Penguin.'

By human standards, this assertion seems incontestable. The emperor penguin's life is an extraordinary feat of endurance in the coldest place on the planet. But the bird, of course, knows nothing else and is supremely well adapted to survive the ordeal. Its tiny, blade-like outer feathers are more tightly packed than any other bird's, and by holding them erect it traps an insulating layer of air in the soft down beneath that keeps body heat in and water out. A thick layer of subcutaneous fat also boosts insulation. Behaviour helps, too: as winter bites harder, birds form a tight huddle that circulates slowly, to ensure that each individual takes its turn at the warm centre.

This is the world's biggest penguin, weighing up to 45 kilograms (99 lb) in peak condition, and the only bird to breed during the Antarctic winter. In March adults trek inland to their colonies on the pack ice, covering up to 120 kilometres (75 miles) – partly on foot and partly by tobogganing on their bellies. After pairs get together, performing elaborate bowing ceremonies, each female lays a single egg, then transfers it carefully on to the feet of her mate, who snuggles it into a fold of warm belly skin. She then returns to the sea to feed, leaving him to incubate the egg alone. For two months this precious cargo remains on the male's feet while he sits out the winter. By late July, it has hatched. The females arrive just in time to take over, regurgitating food for the hatchlings, while their mates, who have not eaten for three months, head for the sea to feed. At seven weeks, with the males now back again, the silver-grey downy youngsters huddle into crèches. Then, at the start of summer (December–January), parents and young migrate en masse to the sea.

In the water, emperor penguins use their streamlined bodies to move with great agility, powered by paddle-like wings. They often hunt by diving below prey – largely fish, krill and squid – in order to spot it against the ice above, then rising to seize it with sharp bill and barbed tongue. They may descend more than 500 metres (1,640 ft), staying down for 18 minutes at a time. Solid bones (unlike those of flying birds) help them to withstand the pressure, and their blood can transport oxygen at low concentrations. Meanwhile non-essential metabolic functions shut down and the heart slows to just 15 beats per minute.

Outside the breeding season, emperor penguins disperse across the Southern Ocean. Satellite tracking has revealed how birds travel more than 2,300 kilometres (1,430 miles) from the colony; in a study in 2006, one individual covered 7,000 kilometres (4,350 miles) in the six months before its tracker gave out. Leopard seals and orcas target young birds. However, climate change poses a much graver threat to the species as a whole; the steady loss of sea ice, caused by the warming of Antarctica – a concept that would have baffled Cherry-Garrard – has depleted food stocks and caused notable declines in key colonies. Today the IUCN lists the emperor penguin as Near Threatened, with an estimated 400,000–450,000 individuals spread across 40 separate colonies.

Wandering Albatross

Diomedea exulans

This enormous ocean-going bird derives its scientific name *exulans* from the ancient Greek for 'exile'. To sailors, its lonely nomadic odyssey on the world's wildest oceans has long struck a chord, hence its significance in maritime folklore. Indeed, in some cultures, the killing of an albatross is an ill omen – as in Samuel Taylor Coleridge's famous poem 'The Rime of the Ancient Mariner', whose narrator courts disaster by doing just this and is forced to wear the dead bird around his neck in penance.

The wandering albatross is the biggest of 22 albatross species, and its 3.1-metre (10 ft) wingspan – occasionally topping a whopping 3.65 metres (12 ft) – is the largest of any bird. Few species are more aptly named: any vessel plying the Southern Ocean can expect to meet this wanderer, angling effortlessly past on its long, narrow wings to who knows where. Its breeding quarters offer only a temporary residence. Most of its life is spent at sea, following the winds and currents to wherever the feeding is most bountiful. In the process, it covers astonishing distances: individual birds may circumnavigate the Southern Ocean three times in a year, covering more than 120,000 kilometres (74,600 miles) at an average of up to 950 kilometres (590 miles) per day.

Like all albatrosses, this species uses a technique called dynamic gliding, in which the high aspect ratio of its elongated wings harnesses the lift from breaking waves, allowing it to remain in the air for hours without expending energy by flapping. Special tendons also lock its wings into their extended position, thus obviating any muscular strain. Other adaptations include a much stronger sense of smell than in most birds, which enables albatrosses to locate their food – squid, small fish and other surface matter – from a great distance. Powerful stomach acids break this food down in their gut, while glands at the base of the bill absorb salt from the system and expel it in a saline solution, visible as a regular drip from the tip of the bill.

Wandering albatrosses mate for life but breed only once every two years. Their colonies are restricted to a handful of southern island outposts, such as South Georgia. A pair starts courtship in early November, with noisy displays of bill-clapping, head-waving, wing-spreading and braying. They build a conical nest mound of mud and vegetation on an exposed ridge, where the breezes assist with take-off. The female lays a single egg in mid/late December, and incubation lasts 11 weeks. Parents alternate roles as their chick grows, one sitting while the other forages, returning to feed their charge on regurgitated stomach oils. The youngster remains in the nest longer than any other bird, not fledging for nearly a year.

After fledging, young birds wander the high seas, not returning to their natal colony for six years and not breeding for 12 or more. Indeed, with a lifespan of up to 60 years, this bird's life cycle takes place over a comparable timescale to our own. Adults have few natural threats. Humans, however, are another matter. Albatrosses often follow fishing boats to scavenge offal and by-catch, and many become snared on longline fishing hooks – which may trail for kilometres – and drown. Plastic waste, often resembling floating carrion, also presents a deadly hazard, especially when it is fed to young back on the nest. Today, with some 26,000 breeding pairs, this species is listed as Vulnerable and, in common with all albatrosses, is the focus of concerted conservation.

Wilson's Storm-petrel

Oceanites oceanicus

A first glimpse of this diminutive seabird fluttering in the middle of a storm-tossed ocean is, for the uninitiated, an alarming sight. You might wonder how something so tiny, with such an apparently feeble flight, could possibly survive the violence of the elements. Indeed, with its superficial resemblance to a house martin (*Delichon urbicum*), you might imagine it to be some migrating land bird blown off-course.

Sailors, however, know these birds to be tougher than they look. The common name 'storm-petrel' combines their apparent fondness for turbulent weather with their signature foot-pattering, which is said to suggest St Peter's attempts to walk over the Sea of Galilee. The traditional nickname 'Mother Carey's chicken' has darker connotations, invoking the supernatural woman feared by sailors and said to be wife to the infamous Davy Jones.

This particular storm-petrel is named after the famous American ornithologist Alexander Wilson (1766–1813) and derives its genus name, *Oceanites*, from the Oceanids, the mythical 3,000 daughters of the Greek goddess Tethys. The most numerous of 25 storm-petrel species worldwide, it is, in fact, one of the world's commonest birds, with a population estimated at over 50 million pairs. That few people have heard of it, let alone laid eyes on one, reflects the remote nature of its lifestyle. Like all its kind, this bird is a true pelagic, nesting in far southern latitudes and spending the rest of its life wandering the world's oceans. It is barely larger than a sparrow, and generally flutters low over the waves, so is hard to spot at sea. Once seen, its white rump, conspicuous against its otherwise sooty-brown plumage, is a prominent identifying feature, while its square tail helps to distinguish it from other storm-petrel species whose tails are forked.

Wilson's storm-petrels breed on remote islands and shorelines around the southern hemisphere, from Cape Horn to the South Shetland Islands, just off the Antarctic Peninsula. Indeed, they are the smallest warm-blooded creature to breed in Antarctica. In early December pairs lay their single egg in a rock crevice or burrow. Incubation lasts around six weeks. Both parents feed the chick, visiting the nest after dark in order to avoid predators. Fledging lasts from 48 days in the southernmost breeding colonies to 78 days at the most northerly, this disparity reflecting the difference in day length between the latitudes.

After breeding, Wilson's storm-petrels head out across the ocean, many gathering in the North Atlantic and some even reaching the Arctic, where they make the most of the northern summer. Like most pelagic birds, their wanderings reflect fluctuations in food and weather. In productive areas, tens of thousands may gather, all fluttering low above the water in search of plankton, krill and other minuscule surface food, dangling their legs as stabilizers while they hang in updraughts from the waves.

This species has a known lifespan of ten years, although, given the impressive ages recorded in other storm-petrel species, it may exceed this. Out on the ocean wave, it has little to fear. Life is more hazardous on its breeding grounds, however, where chicks – and adults returning to feed them – may be targeted by skuas and sheathbills, predatory birds that are clearly prepared to risk the wrath of Mother Carey.

CARIBBEAN

Magnificent Frigatebird

Fregata magnificens

This tropical seabird derives its name from *frégate*, the French word for a small fighting warship. Its traditional English name, 'man-of-war bird', also reflects the bird's belligerent behaviour – in particular, its piratical pursuit of other seabirds, forcing them to abandon their catch. The name appears in the journals of Christopher Columbus from his first voyage across the Atlantic. 'They saw a bird that is called a frigatebird, which makes the boobies throw up what they eat in order to eat it herself,' wrote the explorer, as his ships passed the islands of Cape Verde on 29 September 1492. 'She does not sustain herself on anything else.'

Columbus deserves credit for his observations, but with a couple of caveats. First, the magnificent frigatebird *does* sustain itself in other ways. In fact, its kleptoparasitism – the scientific term for stealing food from other species – may be dramatic to watch but accounts for only a small part of its diet. Otherwise, it uses its long bill to pluck fish, squid and other morsels from the surface of the ocean, sometimes even snatching flying fish as they leap. It never lands on the waves, however, since its plumage lacks waterproofing oils and would quickly become too waterlogged for take-off.

Second, the magnificent frigatebird appears, sadly, to be extinct on Cape Verde. Its breeding range in the Atlantic is now restricted to the *western* side, from Florida through the Caribbean to southern Brazil, and it also occurs at corresponding latitudes in the eastern Pacific, from Peru to Mexico, including on the Galápagos Islands. When not breeding, it ranges much more widely, using its long wings and lightweight build to cover vast distances with minimal effort. Indeed, this species has the lowest wing-loading (the ratio of body weight to wingspan) of any bird, its plumage weighing more than its skeleton. Its ability to remain airborne is rivalled only by swifts (see page 45) and, like swifts, it routinely sleeps on the wing.

This is the largest of five frigatebird species, measuring up to 2.2 metres (7¼ ft) across the wings. Like the others, it has brownish-black plumage and an unmistakable angular flight silhouette, with long, narrow wings and a long, forked tail. Its strangest feature is best seen in the breeding season: a loose 'gular sac' of red throat skin, which displaying males inflate into an outlandish scarlet balloon. Breeding pairs build their large platform nest in a low tree or bush. Incubation of the single egg lasts 55 days, after which both parents work together to feed the chick for its

208

first three months. The male then departs to start another breeding cycle elsewhere, leaving his mate to continue alone for eight more months. And it doesn't end there; after fledging, the chick may remain with its mother for another eight months, thus completing the longest period of parental care known in any bird.

Magnificent frigatebirds face few natural threats, although hunting and rats have taken a toll on some breeding colonies – including, sadly, Cape Verde's. Today the species is listed as Least Concern by the IUCN, and its rakish form, suspended like a child's kite high above the waves, remains a common sight over tropical oceans. Breeding colonies are generally on inaccessible islets, so harder to observe. However, the colony at Codrington Lagoon on Barbuda – the largest in the Caribbean – is now a significant tourist attraction, with boat trips allowing visitors to admire the birds' colourful courtship performances among the mangroves of the lagoon's aptly named Man-o-war Island.

Short-tailed Shearwater

Ardenna tenuirostris

As dusk falls over the Bass Strait between mainland Australia and Tasmania, the surface of the sea swarms with thousands of dark birds scudding low over the waves. These are muttonbirds – or, to ornithologists, short-tailed shearwaters. They move in long lines, each individual gliding fast and low behind the next. Some are heading out to feeding grounds; others, already laden with food, are returning to their chicks.

Babel Island, one of numerous islands in the Bass Strait – and since 1995 owned by the Tasmanian Aboriginal community – gets its name from the clamour these birds make at their nest burrows. Some 2.8 million pairs breed there, in the world's largest single colony. The birds arrive in October, each pair returning to the same burrow. Females lay a single egg that hatches in late January after a 53-day incubation. Both parents then make long feeding trips to provision their chick, covering up to 1,500 kilometres (930 miles) and sometimes abandoning it for a week or so.

In their parents' absence, the chicks survive on fat reserves. They gain weight fast. Indeed, at the point of fledging they may weigh 900 grams (32 oz) – almost twice as much as their parents. This explains the traditional name 'muttonbird': the birds were once harvested in great numbers by indigenous communities around the coastlines of Tasmania and Victoria for their fatty flesh, as well as their oil and feathers. This remains Australia's only wild bird species to be commercially harvested, with a limited take every year under licence.

Short-tailed shearwaters are among the bird world's greatest travellers. After breeding, adults and youngsters alike head north to the rich feeding grounds of the north Pacific, ranging from Japan and Kamchatka east to Alaska's Aleutian Islands. This migration mirrors, in reverse, that of the Arctic tern (see page 78) in the Atlantic, and the distances it covers are almost as great: satellite tagged individuals have clocked up 60,000 kilometres (37,300 miles) in a single year. Migration routes follow weather patterns and food supplies. Recent studies have revealed that many birds first head south to feeding grounds in the Antarctic to fatten up for the journey ahead. They then fly north up the western Pacific, covering 11,000 kilometres (6,800 miles) in just 13 days, before spreading out: some east to feeding grounds off northern Japan and the Sea of Okhotsk; others north to the Aleutians and the Bering Sea. In September they start their return journey, down through the central Pacific – some passing the coast of California – to reach their breeding grounds, completing the journey in as little as 18 days.

Up close, the short-tailed shearwater may not appear remarkable. But this gull-sized, sooty-brown bird is impressively equipped for life on the ocean wave. As with all shearwaters, its stiff, narrow wings enable it to save energy by harnessing the updraught from the waves. They also help it to dive deep below the surface to capture small fish and crustaceans, and flocks often congregate around feeding whales, which corral such food sources into bait balls. These adaptations help to explain the species' success: this is Australia's most numerous seabird, with an estimated 23 million pairs, and listed by the IUCN as Least Concern. However, recent mass die-offs along the Alaska coast have raised fears that its food stocks may be at risk from climate change.

White Tern

Gygis alba

This pure-white tropical seabird goes by several names. In the Seychelles it is known as 'fairy tern', but this risks confusion with *Sternula nereis*, a different species known by the same name that occurs in the southwest Pacific. Elsewhere it is called 'white noddy', 'angel tern' and, in Hawaii – where it is the official bird of Honolulu – *Manu-o-kú*.

Whatever you call it, this is an unmistakable bird, with its snow-white plumage and elegant fork-tailed contours set off by its sharp black bill and large, inky-black eyes. It ranges widely across tropical latitudes, primarily in the Indian and Pacific oceans, where it hunts on the open sea for small fish, squid and crustaceans, diving to take prey from just below the surface, and nests in large colonies on islands and coral cays.

The white tern is unusual among seabirds – indeed, among all birds – in that it doesn't bother with any kind of nest construction, not even the shallow scrape in sand favoured by other tern species. Instead, the female lays her single egg directly on the low horizontal branch of a coastal tree, finding a hollow that keeps it in place. Where such trees are unavailable, it may use rocky ledges or even manmade structures.

Scientists think this minimalist approach may help the white tern reduce the parasite burden that comes with conventional nests. The downside is a vulnerability to tropical storms, and violent winds do sometimes wreck a colony. Should this happen, however, the birds can lay again quickly. Incubation lasts for 21 days, and the single fluffy chick hatches with strong clawed feet that allow a firm grip on its exposed perch. Should they survive these precarious early weeks, adults may reach an impressive 42 years.

White terns have long proved a useful navigation aid for sailors. These birds seldom travel more than 45 kilometres (30 miles) from their breeding colonies, so catching sight of their conspicuous white forms out at sea indicates that land is close. To find it, the captain need only point the boat in the direction the birds take when they return to their nests at dusk.

Like many island seabirds, the white tern has suffered in some regions from the introduction of invasive predators, such as rats and cats. Some traditional island societies once also harvested the bird as food. Nonetheless, it remains a numerous species, with numbers estimated in the hundreds of thousands, and is listed by the IUCN as Least Concern.

Blue-footed Booby

Sula nebouxii

In a dance contest, the ponderous performance of the male blue-footed booby might struggle to earn points. But what his routine lacks in dash, it makes up for in originality. Circling his partner in a slow strut, he raises one foot at a time with exaggerated panache, displaying its vivid turquoise webbing. In a brief burst of drama, he then points his bill to the sky and flares his wings, before resuming the slow-circling foot display, throwing in the occasional gift presentation of a twig. The only judge that counts here is the female. The more colourful his feet, it seems, the higher she scores him.

This tropical seabird of the eastern Pacific is unique among its family in using its feet for sexual display. The colour of these appendages, which varies from pale turquoise to deep aquamarine, is brighter in males than in females, and brightest in younger birds. It derives from carotenoid pigments in the bird's food, and its intensity correlates with the quality of the bird's diet. A male's feet are thus an indicator of his health and, by extension, his fertility – hence females favouring the birds with the brightest.

Blue-footed boobies breed in monogamous pairs in colonies on rocky cliffs and islets. A female lays two eggs, on average, and the pair rotate incubation, using their feet to keep the clutch warm. The chicks hatch five days apart. This is bad news for the second one, whose older, larger sibling bullies it, monopolizing the parental food supply – regurgitated fish – and often leaving it to starve to death. The parents do not interfere; they invest enough resources to rear a single chick, and the second one is just insurance. In bumper food years they might manage to rear both. This brutal breeding strategy, called facultative siblicide, occurs in a few other bird groups, including eagles. Studies suggest that the second chick, should it survive, suffers no long-lasting ill effects – except, possibly, a lifetime of resentment.

This species is one of ten in the Sulidae family, which comprises the boobies of the tropics and the gannets of more temperate latitudes. 'Booby' derives from the Spanish *bobo*, 'fool' or 'clown', and describes the bird's clumsy big-footed walk. Medium-sized, with a wingspan of around 1.5 metres (5 ft), it feeds – like all its family – on shoaling fish such as sardines, capturing them with a dramatic plunge-dive, in which it arrows bill-first into the water from heights of up to 30 metres (100 ft). Special adaptations aid this technique: the forward-facing eyes (a striking pale yellow) allow the binocular vision required to target prey underwater; the nostrils are sealed shut to keep water out; and air sacs in the face and chest cushion the bird against the repeated impact of its dives. Below the surface, it uses its wings to dive deeper and secure its prey. Large fishing parties form where food is abundant, the water appearing to detonate in all directions as many birds dive simultaneously. Such gatherings also attract frigatebirds (see page 208), which may pirate the boobies' catches as they return to feed their chicks.

Blue-footed boobies breed on rocky coasts and islands in the tropical and subtropical eastern Pacific, from Mexico to Peru. The Galápagos Islands are home to their own subspecies, which historically has occurred in great abundance. Sadly, recent years have seen significant breeding failure. Scientists attribute this to the regional disappearance of clupeid fish stocks (sardines and their relatives) following the El Niño event of 1997–8, which wreaked havoc on ocean currents. The species may yet need more than a little fancy footwork to get back on track.

Brown Skua

Stercorarius antarcticus

'The flipper boys – that's you – eat the fish,' says Skua Boss to Mumble the baby penguin in the animated movie *Happy Feet*. 'The flying boys – that's me – eat the flipper boys *and* the fish. And lately,' adds the big brown bird, looming menacingly over our hero, 'there ain't too many fish.'

Yes, the movie may have taken a few liberties: skuas don't speak in a broad Bronx accent, for a start. But in ecological terms, it is spot on. This formidable seabird is an opportunistic predator, fully capable of catching fish but equally adept at making a meal of infant penguins. It is also an inveterate scavenger, hanging around seal colonies to feast on afterbirth or dead pups. In short, if anything edible to a meat-eater appears on the barren shorelines of the Southern Ocean, this bird will be among the first to know.

Happy Feet is set in Antarctica, and indeed this species, also known as the Antarctic skua, has been recorded at the South Pole. But it also ranges more widely across the Sub-Antarctic, finding breeding grounds wherever it finds plentiful food. The Falkland Islands is one such location. With large colonies of penguins, cormorants and elephant seals, this remote archipelago offers plenty to sustain the predator.

Skuas are closely related to gulls. At up to 2 kilograms (4½ lb), the brown skua is the largest of seven species worldwide and well equipped for its predatory and piratical lifestyle, with a hooked bill for tearing flesh and a powerful flight with which to overhaul another bird and steal its food. Females may mate with several males, which work together to protect their combined territory. Nesting birds are notoriously aggressive, dive-bombing intruders and frequently performing the signature skua warning – a skyward stretch of the wings that displays the bold white crescents near the tips. In the Falklands, the two eggs are laid in a grassy hollow. They hatch after a month, later than those of neighbouring birds. This allows the adults to feed their growing chicks on the fledglings of other species.

Happy Feet may not have been great PR for the brown skua. But these bullyboys of Hollywood animation have their admirers among research scientists at remote Southern Ocean outposts, where they can become extremely tame, entertaining observers with their resourcefulness and demonstrating an ability to recognize individual people. Given time, perhaps a Bronx accent is not out of the question.

Where to go next

The best way to learn more about birds is simply to get out and enjoy them. Nothing could be easier, as birds are everywhere: in your garden and local park; along your commute to work; on your seaside holiday. To take things a little further, a quick trawl online through local or national conservation groups will reveal your nearest bird reserves or other promising haunts. For the traveller, every destination offers new birds. It needn't be a specialist birdwatching tour: just being alert to birdlife enriches your experience of any new corner of the world and can illuminate both its nature and culture.

The armchair traveller, meanwhile, can tuck into a wealth of bird literature and, of course, some dazzling coverage of birds on film, from TV documentaries to YouTube clips. And don't overlook museums; some of my earliest bird excitement was fuelled by the Victorian galleries of London's Natural History Museum. Dusty cases of stuffed specimens may now seem anachronistic but they give an insight into how our relationship with birds evolved – and today, of course, most museums offer so much more.

Further reading

I consulted numerous sources while researching this book, both in print and online. As it is not an academic title, I have not provided an exhaustive list, but the following is a selection of publications that I have found an important reference or inspiration over the years, and would recommend to anyone who wishes to read further about birds or who might want to become involved in their conservation.

Atlas of Bird Migration: Tracing the Great Journeys of the World's Birds, Jonathan Elphick (Firefly Books, August 2011)
An excellent, abundantly illustrated book that covers all aspects of this astonishing phenomenon, including individual accounts of more than 500 species.

The Atlas of Birds: Mapping Avian Diversity, Behaviour and Habitats Worldwide, Mike Unwin (Bloomsbury, June 2011)
One of my own. All aspects of the world's birds, from evolution to culture and conservation, are presented through the medium of maps.

Birds Britannica, Mark Cocker and Richard Mabey (Chatto and Windus, 2nd Edition, April 2020)
Detailed and beautifully written species-by-species account of the social and cultural history of birds in Britain.

Birds and Light, Lars Jonsson (Helm, November 2002)
This celebrated Swedish artist captures the essence of birds in a way few other artists have ever rivalled. A dazzling collection.

Birds and People, Mark Cocker and David Tipling (Jonathan Cape, August 2013)
Hefty, sumptuous and encyclopedic exploration of people's relationship with birds around the world, packed with images and personal accounts.

Cornell Lab of Ornithology
(birdsna.org)
Comprehensive online reference for over 760 bird species that breed in North America, with in-depth species accounts, plus sounds, images, video and maps.

Handbook of the Birds of the Western Palearctic, ed. Stanley Cramp et al. (Oxford University Press, September 1994)
Landmark nine-volume ornithological handbook to the birds of Europe, the Middle East and North Africa. An exhaustive repository of information, 20 years in the making, although now overtaken in some areas by more recent science.

Raptors of the World, James Ferguson-Lees and David A. Christie (Helm, January 2001)
The definitive guide to this popular group of birds, covering all 340 species of birds of prey.

The Seabird's Cry, Adam Nicolson, (William Collins, April 2018)
Powerful book from a renowned nature writer that tells the story of ten species of seabird – their life cycles, the threats they face and the passions they inspire.

Twentieth Century Wildlife Artists, Nicholas Hammond (Viking, September 1986)
Birds dominate in this wonderful collection from many of the world's greatest wildlife artists. Explores how our depiction of birds in art reflects our culture and has evolved alongside our knowledge.

Vesper Flights, Helen Macdonald (Vintage, August 2021)
Brilliant, beautiful and thought-provoking essays on our relationships with birds and other aspects of the natural world from a deservedly best-selling nature-writer.

The Life of Birds, David Attenborough (BBC, 1998)
Inspiring ten-episode BBC nature documentary series written and presented by Sir David Attenborough, detailing many aspects of bird behaviour around the globe, much of which had never before been filmed. Available on DVD.

Conservation

The following organizations are all involved in the study and conservation of birds. Many provide a useful source of reference. Some also offer citizen science projects in which volunteers can participate.

Audubon Society
(www.audubon.org)
North America's leading conservation organization, with over 450 chapters across the United States. Promotes the protection of birds, among other wildlife, with publications, wildlife preserves and citizen science projects.

Birdlife International
(www.birdlife.org)
Global partnership of conservation organizations that works to conserve birds, their habitats and global biodiversity. Its online Data Zone (datazone.birdlife.org) is a comprehensive reference to all the world's bird species and their status.

British Trust for Ornithology
(www.bto.org)
UK charity that focuses on the understanding of birds and changing bird populations. Since 1933, the BTO has been working with volunteers to advance ornithology through surveys and monitoring schemes.

ebird (ebird.org)
Online resource that co-ordinates observations from birdwatchers worldwide to create huge data sets that help inform the study and conservation of birds.

IUCN (www.iucn.org)
The International Union for Conservation of Nature. International NGO that gathers data in order to monitor the conservation status of all plant and animal species on Earth. The IUCN Red List assigns each species a conservation category, ranging from Least Concern to Critically Endangered.

RSPB (www.rspb.org.uk)
The Royal Society for the Protection of Birds is the UK's largest nature conservation charity. It lobbies for conservation, encourages citizen science, manages nature reserves and works with numerous international partners to promote bird conservation and research worldwide.

Peregrine Fund
(www.peregrinefund.org)
Non-profit organization founded in 1970 when the peregrine falcon was nearly extinct in North America. Has since extended its work to many raptors around the world, researching little-known species, conserving habitat, educating the public, and building communities' capacity for conservation.

Index

About the illustrator

Ryuto Miyake is an illustrator and graphic designer based in Tokyo. Miyake prefers traditional drawing styles, using acrylic gouache applied with a thin brush on stretched-out watercolour paper, but his detailed illustrations have a contemporary look. His clients include Gucci, Toyota, Frieze and Bottega Veneta. ryutomiyake.com

Author's acknowledgements

I would like to thank all those whose hard work and encouragement lie behind this book. It was a pleasure working with the team at Laurence King. I am grateful to Jo Lightfoot for conceiving and commissioning the project and, especially, to Melissa Mellor, for taking over during a difficult time (when the Covid-19 pandemic was disrupting the world of publishing, along with everything else) and showing great understanding and patience, not to mention impressive editorial expertise, in helping me complete the job. Thanks, too, to designer Masumi Briozzo for her lovely layouts; to copyeditor Rosie Fairhead and proofreader Alison Effeny for their painstaking work; and of course to Ryuto Miyake, for bringing this book to life with his dazzling gallery of illustrations: an amazing achievement, and all done in double-quick time.

I am grateful to all those naturalists and conservationists whose dedication to birds has brought us a deeper understanding of these inspiring animals. Without them, my life would have been a very different and much impoverished one (and I'm not talking about money). Thanks, too, to the friends and companions who have accompanied me on my bird-related travels and adventures around the world. Birds are even better when shared. And thanks, finally, to my own family: my parents, who encouraged my love of all nature from my earliest days; and my wife Kathy and daughter Florence, with whom I have enjoyed many memorable bird moments.